The Manaslu Adventure

Three hapless friends
try to climb a big mountain

MARK HORRELL

"Nothing in the world meant anything, except Everest.
Except the challenge – and the dream.
'All right, let's get at it!' I shouted.
And I thought: 'Yes, at it. Up it. Up it this time – the
seventh time – to the top.'
It must be now –"

Tenzing Norgay

THE
MANASLU
ADVENTURE

Footsteps on the Mountain
Travel Diaries

DAY 1
LEAVING CIVILISATION

Saturday, 3 September 2011 – Soti Khola, Manaslu Circuit, Nepal

The adventure starts at 12.30 on Friday in a place called Dading Besi, about three hours' drive from Kathmandu. Twelve climbers of seven different nationalities sit on benches in the back of a rickety old truck and start the long ride along an atrociously rutted dirt track to Arughat in the Gorkha region of Nepal.

As well as myself, a Brit, we have my two regular climbing partners Mark and Ian, also from the UK; two Americans, Robert and Steve; Robin from Canada; José the Colombian; Karel the Czech; Anne-Mari the Finn; Mila the Russian; and expedition leader Phil Crampton, owner of Altitude Junkies, the expedition operator we're climbing with, an ex-pat Brit living in New York, who spends most of his life in the Himalayas.

I had hoped our ride in the truck would be short, but it ends up providing seven hours of discomfort. A ridge of metal digs into my back every time we go over a bump. I keep hitting my head on the low roof, and after only an hour of driving I have blisters on my thumbs from clinging for dear life to the struts. We face each other on benches along the sides of the truck. Our bags are piled up in front of us, so there isn't much legroom. It would be bad enough without a hangover, but I'm feeling a little fragile after last night's boozing in Kathmandu. My stomach isn't in the best of shape, which is a concern for the people sitting across from me.

Phil sits beside the open back of the vehicle.

'Dude, do you want to come and sit here? You look like you're going to throw up at any moment.'

The truck slides around as the road climbs through jungle, with a steep drop to our right. We are tossed around like a canoe in a gale, and it doesn't help when Steve remarks how bald the tyres are.

We spend around two hours of the journey by the side of the road, waiting for vehicles that have broken down or are stuck in the mud. On one of these occasions I'm able to grab a few minutes' sleep, impossible when the truck is moving. Robert, who owns a motorcycle dealership and knows a thing or two about vehicle mechanics, wanders down the hill to find out what the problem is.

'They've got a broken leaf spring,' he says when he returns.

'Oh, Jesus!' Steve replies.

I have no idea what a broken leaf spring is, but I gather from this exchange that it must be a bugger to fix. I walk to the front of the queue and have a look myself. A truck is hitched up on a jack, with one of its wheels off and various bits of metal lying on the ground underneath. A dozen Nepalis are crouching down, fiddling with the debris. Luckily someone happens to be carrying a spare leaf spring and they get the vehicle moving. We all jump back in our trucks, but only a moment later we grind to a halt when a vehicle in front drives into a ditch. Eventually they get it out and we continue. It's clearly going to be dark by the time we reach Arughat. We reach the bottom of a hill and cross a wide plain among rice fields, but when we start driving up the other side I wonder if we're ever going to reach our destination.

'This place does exist, doesn't it?' I ask Phil.

'Dude, it's unheard of to reach Arughat in one day,' he replies.

This is his third expedition to Manaslu, and on each previous occasion he had to stop somewhere on the way, find porters and walk. This time we make it. Even more surprisingly my stomach survives the ordeal without decorating the back of the truck with its contents.

Porters assembling for work in Arughat

We stay in a lodge instead of pitching tents in the dark. I expect to experience bed bugs during the night – the Manaslu Circuit trek isn't as developed as other parts of

Nepal – but the lodge is very clean, and I get a good night's sleep to make up for last night's binge.

In the morning 150 porters are waiting in the yard behind the lodge, ready to take our 5,000kg of equipment up to base camp. It's more porters than we need, but many are no more than boys, so our Sherpa team have no problem weeding them down to the requisite 102. I watch for a while. Although it looks chaotic, there's no sign of the furious arguments that you sometimes see on the first day of portering.

It's swelteringly hot and still early in the morning when we leave. Arughat is at an altitude of only 610m in a valley between jungle hills. Although there is some cloud cover, when the sun is out it's warm and humid. We set off at around 9.30, and for the first two hours we walk through a sprawl of villages. People cluster in doorways doing little but watch the world go by. They don't see many trekkers around here, and the kids are friendly, running behind us and calling out *namaste* (hello) every step of the way. It's exhausting, but I keep smiling, put my hands together and mutter *namaste* back to them.

We stop for a water break in the shade of a large pipal tree. Robert seems to be good with the kids and they cluster around him. While Mark, Ian and I were out on a Kathmandu bar crawl two days ago, Robert spent his evening at a nunnery orphanage. I ask him about it, and an interesting story emerges that puts us to shame.

'My daughter is a Gurung from a place called Jharkot on the Annapurna trail. We adopted her and took her to America when she was two, which allowed her single mother to remarry and start another family with a new husband. They've since had five kids, and the middle one, a daughter, was put into a nunnery at a young age. It's the

4

tradition in Nepal for the middle kid to become a monk or nun. But she has problems with her eyes. Sometimes the pupils roll right up into the top of her head and you can only see the whites. She has trouble focusing on short and long distances. I think of these people as family, so I wanted to do something to help. We found a specialist ophthalmologist in Kathmandu on the internet, but you can't just show up and take the kid away, so I spent Thursday meeting the nuns for a few hours, talking to them and trying to build their confidence that I really wanted to help this girl. I don't know whether her eyes can be treated, but we have to give it a shot.'

At 11.30, after two hours of walking, we stop for lunch in a grove of trees beside the Budhi Gandaki, the river whose valley we'll be following for the next few days. Our fourteen-strong kitchen crew unpack a mine of steel pans and spread them out across the grass as we stop and chill out for a leisurely two-hour lunch break. I find a comfortable rock to lean against, but have to change position after the sun moves through the branches of a tree and I suddenly find myself in burning heat.

We only have a couple of hours to walk after lunch, but the heat is unbearable and I sweat buckets. I carry my water bottle in my hand so that I can swig regularly. The dirt track is still passable to vehicles for some of its length, but only just. We have to cross the river. A Land Rover is stuck in water nearly up to its bonnet. The truck behind tows it out, and it's able to drive through the deep ford at the second attempt.

It isn't much easier for us. I take my boots and socks off and begin wading in water almost knee deep, but the current is powerful and I find it difficult to stand up on the rocks beneath the surface. Fortunately, Robert, who is walking behind me, lends me one of his trekking poles. With the extra support it's simple enough, but it isn't made any easier by the young kid swimming in the water beside me, who paddles right up and laughs at me. I'm not an aggressive man, but if I didn't need the walking pole I'd be tempted to belt him with it. I wouldn't get washed away by the current if I fell, but my camera would probably be ruined on day one of the expedition, which I wouldn't regard as a fair swap for a small child's entertainment.

I find I've regained my sense of humour a little later when we pass through another village and a small girl starts pointing at me and laughing.

'Monkey, monkey,' she cries. This definitely isn't a friendly greeting, but the sheer bare-faced cheek of it makes me laugh.

I'm not the only one providing entertainment for the local people. An hour later two young porter women walking ahead of me start pointing at Mark and giggling.

'You know why they're laughing,' I tell him afterwards. 'It's because you've got big feet, and you know what they say about people with big feet?'

He ignores me, perhaps wisely.

The two porter girls are young businesswomen who have been following us for a good reason. A short while later we arrive at our campsite at Soti Khola, in two grassy terraces beside the river. They unpack their loads to reveal bottles of Sprite, Fanta, Pepsi, and even some Tuborg beers.

Now I know the real reason they were laughing at Mark. They probably saw 'sucker' written across his forehead.

We sit down under the cover of a shady veranda and are still sweating like pigs. The girls have filled a bucket of river water, and the drinks are sitting there beside us, cooling down. It doesn't take long before all the non-alcoholic drinks have been bought up and gulped down. At 100 rupees a bottle it's been well worth their while carrying their loads all this way, a good day's work for these two young women. And they got to laugh at Mark for good measure.

It's been a hot day under monsoon sun, and we've timed our walk well. At four o'clock, fifteen minutes after we arrive, the heavens open and batter the tin roof of our shelter. The monsoon rain cools things down considerably, but even so I wouldn't fancy putting on an extra layer of Gore-Tex in the heat.

At dinner Phil talks about the influence of monks on Manaslu expeditions. The lama of the monastery in Samagaon, the village at the foot of the mountain, is extremely influential. He decides how much porters from Samagaon get paid (a lot, apparently) and when expedition teams are allowed to conduct their pujas (blessing ceremonies) prior to starting the climb.

This influence goes right back to the early days. The name *Manaslu* translates loosely as 'Spirit Mountain' and is derived from the local word *manasa*, meaning 'spirit' or 'soul'. It took five expeditions before Manaslu was climbed. Bill Tilman was the first man to look for a climbing route when he explored the Annapurna region in 1950. He saw the west face from the Marsyangdi Valley on what has now become the popular Annapurna Circuit trail. He concluded that it was too difficult for his small party to attempt.

Two years later, a Japanese team had a look at both the west and east sides, crossing the Larkya La pass from the Marsyangdi Valley. They thought they could identify a reasonable route up to the summit plateau from Samagaon on the east side.

The Japanese returned in 1953 for the first serious attempt to climb it. They followed the route they had identified the previous year, up to the North Col between Manaslu's north peak and main summit. They reached as high as 7,750m before turning back on their summit attempt because it was getting too late in the day to return to camp safely.

Their next attempt in 1954 was cut short for a more unusual reason. Legend has it that they had to retreat half-naked after an angry mob confronted them at Samagaon, armed with stones and knives. The Japanese were subjected to what in public schoolboy parlance is called a 'de-bagging'. The reason for this humiliation was because the local people believed they had upset the mountain gods by reaching so high the previous year. Soon after they left, an avalanche had destroyed the monastery in Samagaon and killed three monks.

By 1956 things had calmed down a bit. On 9 May, Toshio Imanishi and Gyalzen Norbu Sherpa were positioned in their high camp at nearly 7,800m. They were in good shape for a summit attempt, and set off at the comparatively late time of eight o'clock in the morning.

Finding a slope of blue ice to the left of the summit, they followed a gently undulating snow face to the right. This took them over a series of rocky pinnacles. They climbed one of them believing it to be the summit, only to see another one beyond it. The true summit was a shattered rock tower that was divided from the penultimate summit by a deep gully. The last twenty metres were over rock, and they reached the top at 12.30.

If I do manage to get that far, I guess I'd better not get too excited about any of these summits until I'm absolutely sure I've reached the last one.

Having climbed Makalu with the French in 1955, Gyalzen Norbu Sherpa became the first man to climb two 8,000m peaks. The following day, two of their teammates, Minoru Higeta and Kiichiro Kato, made use of the trail they had broken, and reached the top in just three hours.

While relatively benign in good conditions, the featureless summit plateau takes on a different complexion when the weather closes in. After reaching the summit in 1972 without bottled oxygen, the great Reinhold Messner returned to his camp as a storm blew up. His climbing partner, Franz Jäger, had turned back during their summit attempt. When Messner struggled back to camp, he unzipped the tent to be greeted by the support party of Horst Fankhauser and Andi Schlick, but there was no sign of Jäger. All three of them went out to look for him, but they became lost in the storm and had to shelter in a snow hole. Schlick left the shelter during the night and never returned.

Until recently Manaslu had not been considered a suitable mountain for commercial expeditions. This all changed in 2008, when the Chinese government declined to issue permits for Cho Oyu, across the border in Tibet. Many commercial operators already had clients booked for Cho Oyu, and they didn't want to cancel their expeditions. They turned their attention to Manaslu instead, and have been going there ever since.

Ian and I had both been intending to climb Cho Oyu in 2008 with the British mountaineering company Jagged Globe. When they changed our objective to Manaslu I decided to withdraw from the expedition, but Ian stuck with it. Unfortunately, after six weeks of heavy snow, he had to return home without getting a chance at the summit. Some of his fellow climbers stayed and reached the fore-summit a week later, but with no fixed ropes along the summit ridge to the shattered rock tower, they went no further. Phil was on the mountain at the same time. He led his client Valerie Parkinson to the true summit, and she became the first British woman to climb Manaslu.

I reflect on these stories. Although I've had a few attempts on 8,000m peaks and have never reached a summit, I can count myself lucky that I have never, like the Japanese, returned trouserless from a mountain.

'Those monks, yeah. They can be difficult,' says Phil. 'One year we wanted to start climbing early, but the Sherpas won't go on the mountain until the puja's been done. We wanted to go up the mountain on the day of the puja, and we're sitting there with our harnesses on, but the lama's going on and on, and I'm saying to Tarke, "Can you get this dude to get finished – we need to go."'

We discover that Phil is slightly deaf in one ear, and he's having trouble following our conversation above the roar of the river just beneath our campsite. Mark shouts some comment down the table about asking the lama to check his star charts.

'What's he say?' Phil asks.

'Something about showing him your star charts,' I translate.

'Show him my Johnson?' Phil says. Everybody laughs.

'Somehow I don't think that's going to impress the lama,' Mark says.

We have a civilised meal, which includes red wine, and yet again Mark and I stay up later than everyone else. Had we been in Kathmandu then I dare say it would have been after midnight before the evening ended, but on the first day of the trek our 9.30 turning-in time counts as a late night.

DAY 2
WET, WET, WET

Sunday, 4 September 2011 – Macha Khola, Manaslu Circuit, Nepal

We're supposed to be having a 7.30 breakfast this morning, so I figure that seven o'clock will be a reasonable time to get up. Shortly after the ungodly hour of six o'clock I hear the unmistakeable sound of my tent being dismantled around me. I peer out and see that our Sherpas have taken all the other tents down already, and mine is the last. Despite our agreement to have a 7.30 breakfast, it seems the porters and Sherpas are keen to leave earlier.

By 7.45 we're all packed up, breakfasted and ready to go. Already our narrow valley is out of shade and it's swelteringly hot. Within just thirty minutes of starting to walk I've sweated so much that the sweat is dripping down my brow and into my eyes.

I set off later than the others and walk a little quicker to catch them up.

'Feeling your oats this morning?' Robert says as I overtake him.

'Excuse me?'

'Have you not heard that expression?' he says. 'Horses

eat hay and it makes them strong, so in the States we say "feeling your oats" when you're feeling strong.'

'I see,' I reply. 'I was a bit confused. You see, in the UK we have an expression "getting your oats", but it has a very different meaning.'

'Oh yeah?'

'It means to have sex.'

I can sense the conversation degenerating, through no fault of Robert's. I'm concerned that he may be forming a poor opinion of his new British travelling companions, who spent a night partying in Kathmandu while he was busy helping a teenage nun get treatment for her eyes. So in an attempt to impress him, I tell him a story about the 18th century lexicographer Samuel Johnson, who wrote the very first dictionary of the English language. He famously defined the oat as 'a grain, which in England is generally given to horses, but in Scotland supports the people'.

Basketed porters leave Soti Khola

Despite the heat it's a much nicer walk today now that we're beyond the reach of vehicle access. We're still at a very low altitude, less than 800m. The Budhi Gandaki River cuts through a narrow gorge for much of today's length, with steep jungle hills stretching hundreds of metres above our heads on either side.

At one point we pass a rock pool by the side of the trail, with a heavy waterfall crashing down into it. Some of the group jump in for a dip, but along with my fellow Englishmen I decide to sit in the shade above them and rest. I wouldn't want any of my teammates getting snow blindness from too much lily-white flesh this early in the expedition.

After a couple of hours of walking the valley opens out a little. We pass above terraces of lush green rice fields, with farm cottages dotting the hillsides all around us. It's 10.30, and we stop for lunch at one of the teahouses in a village called Lapubesi. I arrive behind the others. By now the full length of my trouser legs are dripping in sweat and as wet as a salmon's cardigan. The team are sitting underneath a sheltered veranda, and everybody laughs at me when I go to sit down.

'I can't take this heat. I'm a Yorkshireman. What are you trying to do, kill me?' I say to Phil.

Lunch takes three hours as we wait for the kitchen crew to arrive, unpack all their kit and cook a hot meal. This is the sort of leisurely stop that drove me mad when I trekked in Nepal in the autumn season last year. It would be a lovely sunny morning when we stopped for an early lunch. By the time we left a few hours later the sun had invariably fallen asleep behind a cloud. Later in the afternoon it usually rained. My climbing partner Mark and I sometimes ignored the kitchen crew when we saw them unpacking for lunch. We kept on walking so that we could get to our campsite before the heavens opened and we suffered a drenching. But it was just two of us then. In a group of ten climbers I have to go with the flow – others might enjoy a hot meal and a long break.

In the afternoon the valley narrows again and we continue along a dramatic path hewn into a rock face high above the river. The sun has moved around, and the towering hills and cliffs keep us in shade.

There are fewer villages today, but we do pass a school where, once again, I find myself a source of entertainment for the children. As I walk past, half of them scream *namaste, namaste* at me, while the other half scream 'monkey, monkey'. When this happened yesterday I laughed, but now I know the reason for it I'm not so happy. Earlier in the day we saw some grey langur monkeys climbing in the trees. They had silver manes and white faces. This isn't a friendly greeting, but a heckle for the white-skinned foreigner. Perhaps I'm paying the price for centuries of cultural oppression, but a truckload of abuse from a playground of rowdy schoolkids doesn't add to my enjoyment of the trek, so I increase my pace and ignore them.

The path eventually descends to the riverbed through trees, and we have to wade across a couple of side channels. I take my boots and socks off to cross the first. The water comes halfway up my thighs and wets my rolled-up trousers, but the stream bed is made of soft sand and is kind on my bare feet. The second channel consists of jagged rocks. I wander a few metres and it feels like I'm walking on hot coals. I clench my teeth, but the soles of my feet are in too much pain. It takes for ever, and I end up putting my boots back on to wade across. I'd rather have wet shoes than feet that have been cut to pieces. I have to hope my boots will dry out by the fire tonight.

Shortly afterwards the heavens open, and we complete the last half hour of today's walk under the full force of monsoon skies. We arrive soaking wet at the village of Macha Khola, at an elevated position in forest above the gorge. We're able to take shelter in a teahouse, where we hang out our saturated clothing. It's another two hours before the rain stops and we're able to put up the tents, but I don't think our clothes will ever get dry.

DAY 3
THE BACK END OF A HORSE

Monday, 5 September 2011 – Jagat, Manaslu Circuit, Nepal

I wake up this morning to the sound of Phil's voice outside my tent.

'"Yo, motherfucker" – that's Mark Horrell's impression of an American, isn't it?'

I can hear him despite wearing ear plugs. I remove them and poke my head out. Once again, most of the tents have already been taken down and mine is among the last. All things are relative, but it's clear that in this team I'm not an early riser. It's still only six o'clock – a good time to get up and start walking before the sun gets too hot. I go through the unpleasant process of putting on my wet clothes from the previous day. Worst of all are my boots, which are still saturated from my wade through the Budhi Gandaki.

Today is not as bad as the previous two. The sides of the gorge are higher here, and although we set off at the same time, we're in shade for nearly an hour. We spend most of the morning stuck behind pack mules. The narrow path weaves around a cliff face some distance above the river, and it's sometimes difficult – not to say dangerous – to slip past. I round a corner and see Karel climbing up through the undergrowth below the path. He seems a little shaken, and it's not surprising – he tried to squeeze past a mule and was pushed off. I look down. Luckily the thick undergrowth cushioned his fall, but had it not been there he would have been dashed to smithereens on the riverbed dozens of metres below.

On a high trail through a forested gorge

Every so often the path drops to a wider shelf, and a long line of us leg it past a longer line of mules, but within minutes we find ourselves behind the next lot. After about three hours of this we arrive at a teahouse by the side of the trail. There's a grim paved area in front, but also some shade. We rest for nearly an hour while we wait for all the mules to get a good distance ahead of us.

Phil claims that he performed a good deed by leading from the front as we followed the horses. He tells us that he kept getting 'blow back'.

'Man, I don't want to be stuck behind a horse's ass all the way till lunch,' he says.

'But I thought Mark was behind you, not in front,' I reply.

'There's only one way to reply to that, but no one has a snare drum and a cymbal,' Mark says.

We reach our lunch stop about an hour later: another teahouse with a dirt yard at the front. I haven't sweated as much this morning as I have on previous days. This isn't just because I've been stuck behind the back end of a horse, but because quite a lot of the walk has been in shade.

Lunch brings a welcome opportunity to dry my boots and socks while we wait for our food to arrive. Mark pulls out a large lens for his camera because Phil says we're likely to see monkeys on the walk this afternoon.

I talk to Anne-Mari, who became the second Finnish woman to climb Everest. Last year she was in a race with another woman to be the first. They were climbing the mountain at the same time, but Anne-Mari decided there wasn't a good weather window on the day her rival chose to go for the summit. She sacrificed priority for a safer summit day – a wise decision that will only be disputed by those who put bragging rights before experience. She's very slight, but she's super fit. She's always at the front of the group, and her blonde hair and bronzed limbs look like they could keep going for ever. I ask her what she does for a living, and the answer seems to be not much. She lives with her husband in Dubai for most of the year, works for about three months in a bar back in Finland, and for the rest of the year she runs marathons, half-marathons, and cross-country races. She is one of Finland's top marathon runners. She receives enough money in sponsorship to maintain her lifestyle and do a few mountaineering expeditions for good measure.

Anne-Mari is not the only Everest summiteer in our party – Karel the Czech has also climbed it, as have Phil and all our climbing Sherpas. And then there's Robert, who climbed above the Balcony (at 8,400m on Everest's South-East Ridge) before deciding to turn around.

By contrast, the three Brits have been rather less successful on the 8,000ers. Mark has attempted Cho Oyu, Gasherbrum II and Everest, but illness or avalanches thwarted him on each occasion. Ian has been on expeditions to Manaslu and Gasherbrum II, but snow conditions prevented him from attempting the summit. Meanwhile I have tried Gasherbrum I, Gasherbrum II and Cho Oyu, but I've barely made it higher than 7,000m. My reasons for failure have been many and varied; I'm half-expecting to arrive in Samagaon and – like the Japanese – be told to proceed naked.

Lunch takes just two hours today, and we're away again before two o'clock. At last we have some ascent after sweating away at low altitude for the last two and a half days. We climb about 300m as the river rises to arrive at a wide, grassy flood plain. The scenery is spectacular. Cliffs tower above us on either side, overgrown with tropical vegetation. By three o'clock the sky has clouded over and I keep expecting the usual afternoon downpour, but it doesn't happen and the walk is very pleasant.

At 4.30 we arrive at a teahouse in Jagat, a village that seems to suffer from a plague of giant insects. For once I feel quite dry, but when all the kit arrives, the tents get erected and I put on some genuinely dry clothes, I realise that everything I was wearing is as sodden as ever. This means I'll be putting it on wet again tomorrow morning.

DAY 4
PARADISE ENCLOSED

Tuesday, 6 September 2011 – Deng, Manaslu Circuit, Nepal

I'm slower getting up this morning, yet again. No sooner do I climb out of my tent than Tarke starts taking it down. I take out my pee bottle to empty in the bushes, and instinctively offer it to him.

'Would you like some juice, Tarke?' I ask.

He winces in repulsion and turns away, but then he roars with laughter in that raucous way Sherpas all seem to do.

Every day of this trek seems to be better than the last, and today is no different. We rise up the left-hand side of the valley high above the Budhi Gandaki River on a dramatic pathway of rock steps. The valley widens into grassy folds, and on the opposite side we see our first snow-capped peak of the expedition. Shringi Himal (7,161m) leaps up miles above everything else, its flanks partly sheathed in cloud.

We have now entered the Manaslu Conservation Area. The few villages we pass through seem much cleaner, although a part of one of them has been wiped out by a vast – and recent – landslide. We boulder hop across gigantic rocks the size of houses. A sea of dark earth has flattened several fields of maize. Landslides are regular hazards in these parts, especially at this time of year during monsoon season. We can only hope there were no human casualties, but it's hard to see how anyone living in its path would be able to survive such a catastrophic event.

We reach a grove of trees beneath a long suspension bridge over the river. Here we stop for some shade. There's a tiny police checkpoint, and Phil has to get our permits stamped. As we stop and wait we attract the attention of blue-uniformed schoolchildren on their way to school up the hill in the village of Philim. A small yappy dog pesters a big lazy one lying in the sun. It snaps its jaws repeatedly, but eventually the big dog decides to get up and show who's boss. It grabs the hind leg of the small one in its jaws and pulls it over. The small dog is forced into a submissive posture, on its back with its four legs spread apart. The big dog continues to scratch at its belly with its teeth. We watch in fascination as it looks like it's about to start fellating it.

'Isn't that illegal?' Mark says. 'I'm sure those two dogs are related.'

We cross the river and climb up to a high trail which contours around the hillside. We have lunch in a wooden shack beside the trail in a place called Eklebhatti. I wait for an hour watching chicks and hens peck around beside my feet, then fall asleep in the sun. I'm woken for lunch an hour later.

The afternoon's walk is breathtaking. We start off in hot sun on a narrow path to the right of the river. We overtake porters all along as the path widens. Then we cross to the other side of the river, and the gorge narrows even further. In some places it is no wider than thirty metres, with steep cliffs rising on either side. Yet it's still thickly wooded. We trek through pine forest on narrow rock-hewn paths some distance above the river. It reminds me of the Naar Phu Gorge in the Annapurna region not far from here. That was one of my favourite ever places when I walked up it three years ago, and I felt privileged to be there.

We reach Deng at 3.30, a cluster of wooden shacks at a confluence of gorges. A stupa arch and prayer flags remind us that we've arrived in the land of the Buddha. A small ledge about 100m above the river is enough for half a dozen houses and a few fields of maize and cabbages. One of the fields has just enough space for our tents, and we stop after a hard but very satisfying day's trekking. Once again I'm soaked in sweat – but we've climbed to 1,800m today and things will be cooler from now on. The monsoon rains have been absent today despite the cloud cover. This is a fabulous trek. Many Manaslu expedition teams fly to Samagaon by helicopter, and I'm so glad that we're walking there instead.

At dinner we discuss cleanliness. The 24-year-old Mila from Russia has been managing to find somewhere to wash when she arrives in camp each afternoon. She has even brought enough tops to wear a clean one every day. The more battle hardened among us have been putting on the same sodden kit every morning, and changing into something dry when we arrive in camp without bothering to get washed. We feel proud of ourselves, until Phil announces that above base camp he will be using the same Nalgene bottle for peeing that he uses for drinking.

I know it's useful to cut down on excess weight when you have to carry it up a mountain, but I draw the line at this. The thought makes me wince, and Phil hasn't finished.

'When it's dark in my tent at night, I can't see which bottle's which. I sometimes end up drinking from my pee bottle, so I figured I could just use the same one for both.'

'Why don't you use a wide-necked Nalgene bottle for peeing and a narrow-necked one for drinking? Then you can easily tell the difference, even in the dark,' I say.

'The problem for Phil is that he's able to use the narrow-necked one for pissing into as well,' Mark says.

We roar with laughter.

Later in the evening Phil tells us about the time he attended a fancy-dress party dressed as Austin Powers.

'I'm surprised you needed to dress up for that,' Mark says.

We roar again.

Phil has an unusual 1970s haircut, which parts around the sides of his head like the 17th-century monarch Charles I. It looks like he's sporting a pair of springer spaniel's ears, and it often makes him a figure of fun at meal times.

I expect we'll be according our expedition leader more respect when we get onto the mountain.

DAY 5
ENCHANTED FOREST

Wednesday, 7 September 2011 – Namrung, Manaslu Circuit, Nepal

For once I'm up bright and early, at 5.30, and climb out of my tent to find all the other ones still pitched. The porters seem keener than ever to leave early, so much so that some of them leave with empty drums, before we've had time to take down our tents and pack them inside. One of our crew has to run and catch up with them, but it doesn't end there. During breakfast, after the rest of the porters have gone, Phil notices that one of the drums has been left behind. Our sirdar Dorje puts on his pack, slings the drum over his shoulders and sets off after them. He's not happy, and I wouldn't want to be the guilty porter when Dorje overtakes.

Today's walk continues in as dramatic a fashion as yesterday, but there's a lot more ascent – the path climbs up and down, weaving left and right as it goes. It gradually eases its way up the contours of the gorge, every so often dropping to cross a side stream, then rising back up again. Phil leads the way at a stiff pace that I struggle to keep up with on the uphill sections. Luckily, for the first couple of hours there is shade from the hills and many groves of trees along the way. I still sweat like a pig, though.

The path winds high above the river, affording great views up the valley. The land is pleasant and green, with patches of pine wood and steep rocky outcrops rising high above the hilltops. Occasionally we pass cottages of wood and slate surrounded by wheat fields cut in terraces. Now that we're in Buddhist territory we pass many chortens and mani walls.

We continue relentlessly for over two hours and soon find ourselves in hot sun. When it becomes clear that Phil isn't intending to stop, I abandon my attempt to keep up. I find a nice lofty perch beside the trail in the shade of some trees, and stop to rest. I gulp down a large quantity of water, and relax with a fine view up the valley as I watch the others disappear ahead of me.

I catch up with them at 10.30 in the village of Ghat, where we stop for lunch in the cramped courtyard of a run-down, smoky teahouse. A silly conversation takes place about iPhone apps when I start talking about Google Goggles. This particular app takes a photo from your phone and uses sophisticated recognition technology to run a Google search on what it thinks the photo depicts.

'Is there an app called Beer Goggles, which takes a photo of a beer bottle and tells you where the nearest bar is?' Phil says.

'No, Beer Goggles makes someone of the opposite sex look attractive after a few drinks,' Mark replies.

Phil and Mark then have a serious discussion about a potential Beer Goggles app that takes someone's photo and matches it against a database of good-looking movie stars to find the one they most resemble. They are convinced there must be a market for it.

There are other subjects I don't feel like discussing with my companions. After several days of putting on wet clothing every morning, then walking for a few hours in searing heat, sweating profusely, I have what you might call a chafed undercarriage. When I sit down for lunch, I can only guess how much salt is deposited. When we set off to walk again, it's really quite abrasive, and I feel like I'm sandpapering my genitals with every step. I end up walking in bandy-legged fashion to minimise the chafing. It doesn't help when the others shoot off again at a super-fast pace.

It's time for a reality check, and the person to provide it is Karel, who starts at the front of the group but drops back as the others overtake him one by one.

'It seems we have a team of runners,' he says as I pass. 'They go so fast that they see nothing. Nobody is taking photographs; they are missing everything. I arrive to lunch forty-five minutes after you, but I am not sweating and I see everything.'

He's right. One of the reasons I'm sweating so much is that I stopped to take photographs, and then raced to catch up. But we walked for three hours this morning, then had a three-hour lunch break, so there was really no need to go so fast. Karel is one of our Everest summiteers; it's not like he can't keep up, but he knows better.

I follow behind him for a while, and it's clear that here is a man who enjoys the whole experience of being in the mountains, and is not just here to bag the summit. At one point I see him stop to examine the ground. He picks something up and walks with it in his hand for a few metres before gently setting it down on a rock. When I stop to see what had so delighted him, I see a beautiful many-coloured butterfly sunning its wings.

The trail passes deeper into forest as the river narrows. It seems impossible it could get any narrower. At its zenith it squeezes between clashing rocks in a series of noisy cascades. We've crossed some very long footbridges in the last few days, but the wooden bridge that spans the river here is barely ten metres long. It looks right over a natural bridge of rock above one of the waterfalls – the gorge is now so narrow that it seems like the cliffs on either side are reaching out to touch one another.

We cross the narrows for a second time, then ascend into mixed forest of pine, bamboo and rhododendron. I stop to let a train of pack mules past in the other direction, and get out my camera to video them. When the muleteer passes me at the back of the train and sees me filming him, he plays up to the camera, leaping around like a chimpanzee.

But if I think he's the only performer then I'm in for a surprise. When I stop to let a second train of mules pass a little later, I look up to see that the muleteer at the back has his mobile phone out and is busy filming me.

I'm reminded of the explorer Bill Tilman's reaction to the Nepalis he met in the village of Manang, not far from here in the Annapurna region, when he travelled there in the 1950s. Tilman thought he was travelling into a primitive world of unsophisticated villagers, and expected them to regard him with greater respect than he was afforded at home. He was disappointed when, 'a man whom we attempted to photograph retorted by whipping out a camera himself.'

Fortunately, things have moved on since Tilman's time, and my own response to a similar incident is to laugh – although I resist the temptation to jump around like a monkey myself.

It's a relaxing climb, and I enjoy strolling through the forest on my own. Earlier in the day Phil described this forest as magical. He conjured up an image of enchantment, then butchered it by saying in his usual clowning, buffoonish way that, 'there's elves and pixies and unicorns and everything!'

There's no doubt walking through this primeval forest, with occasional glimpses back down the gorge, has a magical quality to it. The only thing better would be to actually see some of the monkeys Phil's been promising for the last few days.

Clearly nobody else has seen any either, for when I arrive in camp at Namrung, Phil looks up and points at me.

'Look, there's one, everybody – look, there's a monkey.'

Hilarious.

We're all in stitches again later in the evening. Phil and Steve talk about one of the characters in their Manaslu team two years ago, a vocal American who turned out to be an ace base camp manager.

'He was a super nice guy,' Steve says, 'but from what I can gather his neighbours hated him. He was the neighbour from hell. In fact, he was so bad the local fire chief threatened to burn his house down.'

DAY 6
INTO THE HEART OF BUDDHIST COUNTRY

Thursday, 8 September 2011 – Samagaon, Manaslu Circuit, Nepal

Today is all about minimising trouser chafe. Another day of sweating profusely and rubbing salt into already tender parts is going to be painful, so my plan is to execute the slow plod to reduce the risk of sweating and lessen the rubbing. The fact that we're now at high altitude helps. Today we climb from 2,600m to 3,500m, so it's definitely time for slow plodding anyway, to prevent altitude sickness.

We set off from Namrung at 7.20. This time the valley is wider and we start on the western side, so we find ourselves in sun early on. I drop behind the others almost immediately and climb slowly through pine forest on a wide trail that zigzags high above the valley. After 300m of climbing, the trail levels out at a village. Beyond this I contour gently downhill on a path that alternates between sun and shade as it diverts around a side valley.

It's about nine o'clock, and many of the porters who started out first thing in the morning have decided this shaded area is a good place to have breakfast. We must have employed a considerable chunk of the population of Arughat; many are women who have no difficulty carrying loads as big as those of the men. There's a real community feel to these rest breaks, with dozens of porters stopping together. Some of the younger women hitch their skirts up to wash their feet and legs in a stream, while an old man lights a fire and heats a mountain of rice in a huge pot. Usually they ignore us as we pass, but occasionally someone barks a phrase at me in Nepali with a big grin on their face. Whether they're being friendly or making fun of me for the benefit of their companions I have no idea, but I always smile back and reply with a *namaste*.

Passing a Buddhist stupa on the trail

We're in the heart of Buddhist country now, with many stupas, mani walls and tiny gompas. We stop for lunch at a very basic teahouse in Lho, a village in a saddle surrounded by fields. Ian tells us that his helicopter had to make an emergency landing in a wheat field here when he tried to climb Manaslu three years ago.

After lunch the trail continues relentlessly through forest. I'm a long way behind the others now, and in some discomfort. I continue onwards through a filthy village of stone cottages where several new teahouses are being built.

Somewhere up to my left is Manaslu. The alpine nature of the landscape is emphasised when I cross a white waterfall on a narrow wooden footbridge. A mass of water tumbles beneath me, throwing up a ton of spray, and I'm engulfed by its icy blast. It's absolutely freezing, and I'm glad to get over to the other side; it's the first time in a week that I've felt cold, and it was *really* cold.

I crest a rise and look down across a wide plateau. Halfway across it I see a large blue-roofed school, and at the back of the plateau is a community of buildings beneath a small monastery high on a hill. Beyond this I can see a wall of glacier-eroded rock disappearing into cloud. The village is Samagaon, our home for the next three nights as we get acclimatised to the altitude. Manaslu must be up there in cloud, but it looks like we'll have to wait until tomorrow to get our first look at it.

As I approach the village I catch up with Robert, the only person in the team who seems to be as slow as I am. He tells me that his knee is giving him some trouble.

'Well, I'm suffering from trouser chafe,' I reply. 'Very tender underneath.'

He laughs. 'Well, I'm glad I'm not suffering from that particular problem.'

Samagaon is a picturesque village, but quite mediaeval. Terraces of slate-roofed wooden houses cluster behind muddy courtyards. Chickens run around like unsupervised children. Dirty-faced villagers sit on verandas in front of their homes, looking out at us, and a wizened old woman carrying a basket on her back passes by, stooped beneath her load. Still, she is cheerful and greets us with *namaste.*

'Have you ever seen the film *Fiddler on the Roof*?' Robert asks. 'There's a scene at the end set in the dirtiest, most run-down hole of a village in Russia, with mud all over the place. People in rags pushing carts around. Man, it's disgusting. This place reminds me of that scene.'

I was thinking the reverse. I might not want to live here myself, but I enjoy places like this – places that are unspoilt and retain their original character. For their inhabitants the conditions are what they're used to, and just because it seems terribly poor to us westerners, it doesn't mean the people here are not happy.

'I quite like this place,' I reply.

Robert appears thoughtful, but he accepts my statement with a shrug. 'Then I guess we're different.'

We arrive at four o'clock and take rooms in a lodge rather than camping again. I share a room with my British pals Mark and Ian. We quickly fill the whole of one wall with our wet gear hanging out to dry. With two rest days ahead of us I'm looking forward to wearing dry clothes for the first time in a week.

Before long I'm upstairs in a comfortable dining room, drinking Tuborg beer. Sarki our cook has got hold of some yak meat and we have pepper steak and chips for dinner, washed down with a glass of red wine. It's taken us six days on foot from the roadhead to get here, but there's no reason why we can't be civilised.

DAY 7
DAMP MIST AND WINE

Friday, 9 September 2011 – Samagaon, Manaslu Circuit, Nepal

Today is the laziest of lazy days. Phil jokes that I spend the whole of it sitting in the same place at the dinner table, alternately reading and writing. He's not far wrong, though I do spend a couple of hours in the afternoon napping in our bedroom.

There was a brief spell of sunshine first thing in the morning, and I'm told that at 6.30 Manaslu's twin peaks could be seen rising above the village. Phil shows me a photo he took soon after waking up, but by the time I rise at 7.30 it's clouded over again. By ten o'clock the cloud has descended to the village; for most of the day the place is engulfed in an unpleasant fug of moisture, with occasional spells of light rain. It's not a day that tempts me out of doors to explore my surroundings.

Phil thinks he's made the mistake of sending all the wine up to base camp 1,400m above us, but some time during the afternoon he announces that he's found a cask among the several tons of expedition equipment still left down here at Samagaon. So at four o'clock we assemble in the dining room for cheese and red wine. This gathering merges into dinner, and it's a pleasant way to spend an expedition rest day.

DAY 8
MEDIAEVAL VILLAGE

Saturday, 10 September 2011 – Samagaon, Manaslu Circuit,
Nepal

A raucous gathering of villagers assembles in the courtyard of our lodge first thing this morning. We're to send fifty 30kg loads up to base camp today, which means more employment for the villagers. The amount of equipment, and consequently the number of porters that we need, is staggering. We have 5,100kg of gear from the start, and we'll be replenished with more food later in the expedition. We needed 175 porters to carry this up the Budhi Gandaki Gorge from Arughat – 102 of them came with us, and seventy-three came with the rest of our climbing Sherpas a few days earlier. Sixty-eight porters from Samagaon transported the first instalment up to base camp a few days ago; we employ fifty today, with more to follow when we leave for base camp tomorrow.

In the morning the weather is more inviting, though cloud still hangs over Manaslu, which I'm yet to see. Phil leaves for base camp with some of the Sherpas and kitchen crew to begin setting up camp. There's a lot of work for them to do, digging out pitches, not only for our personal tents but for the support tents: kitchen, dining, storage, communications, and toilet and shower tents. It will take them a couple of days, but most of it should be done by the time we arrive tomorrow.

Mark and Robin decide to go for an extensive acclimatisation walk some distance up to base camp. Mila says she will follow them up to a small lake on a hill where she intends to have a swim. If all of this seems crazy enough, I believe Anne-Mari caps it all by going for a run. Most of us continue to take it easy, though.

For me these early days are all about resting, but I'm a little more active than I was yesterday. I go for a wander around the village for a closer look at the houses. Nearly all of them, apart from the few trekkers' lodges at the top end of the village, are built in an identical style. Two-storey stone buildings with slate roofs have a living area on the top floor and storage space underneath for animals and – more often – firewood. A stepladder leads from the ground at the front up to the living quarters, and usually there's some sort of veranda where clothes are left to hang. All of the houses are enclosed by a small yard at the front where long, cut grass is left to dry in the sun.

The village is altogether a pleasant spot surrounded by wooded hills, and the huge mass of Manaslu lurks in cloud somewhere high above. The lives of these people must still be quite primitive, but should more people come to trek the Manaslu Circuit, I can see Samagaon developing into a tourist hub in the way Manang has on the Annapurna Circuit, with bakeries, lodges and even a basic cinema. Whether this is a good thing is a matter of opinion, but it's inevitable that villages like this will be touched more and more by the world beyond – and the villagers are likely to be glad of the opportunities, even if it means their way of life will change.

I alternate my afternoon between snoozing in our room, writing up my diary and reading in the dining room. It's busy in the lodge today and we have to share the place with a large group of Japanese climbers. Many of them seem to be elderly, but there's one young woman too. We are served dinner late, at nearly eight o'clock; Karel and José both miss it due to illness. Robert also says he's not feeling great, but he tries to force down as much food as he can. We have a big ascent tomorrow; I hope they are feeling better by the morning, but there will be plenty of time on the expedition for them to recover.

Grass dries in the yard of a home in Samagaon

DAY 9
CLIMBING WITH PORTERS

Sunday, 11 September 2011 – Manaslu Base Camp, Nepal

We have a long ascent today and a big jump in altitude. From the teahouse at 3,500m in Samagaon, where we've spent the last three nights, we'll be climbing all the way to Manaslu Base Camp at 4,900m. This is a significant altitude gain for a single day. I'm expecting to experience headaches when I arrive.

Our cook Sarki provides us with a packed lunch, and we leave together at 8.30. The path meanders along the flat for the first twenty minutes or so, twice crossing the Budhi Gandaki. The once-mighty river that we followed for six days has now become a narrow if powerful mountain stream.

After a short while the path turns to the left and begins climbing through rhododendron-clad hillsides. It meanders into forest as it becomes steeper, and I drop well behind the others. I've decided the best way to cope with the sudden altitude gain is by indulging in trekker's plod rather than climber's rush. This involves walking as slowly as possible without actually falling over. Two things to avoid at high altitude are overexertion and dehydration, so my aim is to complete the whole ascent without getting out of breath. It's sunny in the early stages of the climb, yet my slow pace means that I don't work up a sweat.

My teammates disappear into the distance ahead of me, but I don't climb alone. I find myself walking at the same pace as our porters, who are carrying loads of 30kg or more.

The path rises out of woodland and I look down on a grey-turquoise lake, Birendra Tal, which remains below me for a long time. I slant uphill across grassy moorland in the direction of a dirty glacier, crossing many streams on stepping stones and rudimentary log bridges. I climb alongside the glacier for a short while on a muddy hillside, then rise above the vegetation zone at about 4,500m.

At this point I see that I'm about to enter thick cloud, so I stop to put my Gore-Tex jacket on and nibble at a last snack. The remainder of the walk follows a narrow ridge of moraine. I know I'm getting close when unladen porters start running past me on their way back down.

The end arrives sooner than I expect. At one o'clock my altimeter is reading 4,750m, and I think there is still another 150m ahead of me when I start passing tents. There are lots of them, including large dining tents. It must be base camp.

After another five minutes I see Phil, and walk into our own camp. All my teammates are busy unpacking. They arrived an hour and a half ago, but had to wait for the tents to be pitched and for the porters to arrive with our duffle bags. I've timed my walk perfectly.

It's still quite mild, and I hear the patter of rain on my tent as I unpack. We're not yet high enough for the rain to fall as snow. My GPS reads 4,840m, very low for base camp on an 8,000m peak, but this means we should be comfortable – if only the weather would improve.

It rains solidly for the next two hours as I get warm and comfortable inside my tent. It has a fitted carpet, a nice touch that gives my accommodation a luxury feel. I think I'm going to be happy here at base camp.

DAY 10
PUJA

Monday, 12 September 2011 – Manaslu Base Camp, Nepal

Today is a day of waiting. It rains for almost all of it. Occasionally the rain is heavy, occasionally a shard of light bursts through; but most of the time a miserable grey drizzle pervades the camp and keeps the mountain hidden from view. This leads me to announce at breakfast that my first aim of the expedition is to see Manaslu; then I'll think about climbing it. It should be easily achievable, but we're now eleven days out of Kathmandu and I'm yet to do so.

At some point today we're supposed to have our puja – the Buddhist ceremony to ask the mountain gods for safe passage – but we don't know when. Monks came up from the monastery in Samagaon early in the morning. For three hours from seven o'clock onwards, we hear the incessant beating of a drum in the camp next door. One of the neighbouring teams is having their puja before us. As a rule of thumb, the bigger the mountain, the longer the puja, and if it's taking three hours then the monks must think conditions are serious.

We do a few odd jobs around camp while we wait for our turn. The Sherpas build a huge platform for our flagpole and altar. Some of us spend the morning litter picking. Whoever used our camp last year didn't bother cleaning up when they left. There's trash all over the place, and picking it up from cracks in the moraine is a meticulous process. They also dumped the remainder of their food; a disgusting mass of some white mushy substance is piled on the ground behind my tent, and although it will biodegrade in the long run, it's going to take a long time at this altitude. In the meantime it's thoroughly unpleasant. We bury the food in earth and rocks so that it's out of sight and out of mind.

That some people leave trash like this lying around is frustrating enough. More frustrating still is that they have been allowed to get away with it. All expedition teams pay a fee to the Government of Nepal for a liaison officer to accompany the expedition. The liaison officer is supposed to travel with the team and help out with any cultural issues. Another of their responsibilities is to ensure that teams obey the rules – such as packing up when they depart from camp without leaving any garbage lying around. But hardly any liaison officers ever do the job they are hired for. Most pocket their fee and stay in Kathmandu; an example of the blatant government corruption that Nepal is well known for.

Our puja starts at one o'clock while we're having lunch. This is a good thing, because it means we can miss the first part, and don't have to sit through a full three hours of chanting. It rains for most of the ceremony. The Sherpas have rigged up a plastic sheet as a makeshift roof, and the monks can chant in the dry. There are three monks seeing to our spiritual salvation: a drummer, a chanter who plays the cymbals, and a little old man with a dog, who sits on the end smiling and occasionally rings a small bell.

I've been to a few pujas now, and it's easy to regard them as a bit tedious. There are two main schools of thought. Some would say that at best they're a lot of old nonsense, and at worst a cynical way of using local superstition to extract money from foreigners. They have to be endured because the Sherpas won't set foot on the mountain without them. More generous folk will say that three monks – who have more important spiritual matters to concern themselves with down in Samagaon – have climbed 1,400m up a difficult pathway to conduct a three-hour ceremony on our behalf, because they're genuinely concerned about our safety. While many westerners will go with the first option, I find that three hours pass by more quickly if you accept the second one, so that's what I do.

In any case, there is a more fun part at the end of the ceremony, when we have to drink alcohol. Tarke brings round a bottle of rum and makes me drink three shots for luck. Then one of the other Sherpas brings a bottle of Royal Stag whisky, and I have to drink three shots of that as well. Then Tarke brings the rum around again. I wonder how long this is going to go on. It doesn't really feel like the time or the place to get steaming drunk, but at least we can now head up the mountain as soon as we're sufficiently acclimatised.

If today's food is anything to go by then I'm going to be losing a lot of weight on this expedition. We're served a breakfast of stodgy pancake with rock-hard chocolate spread, and we're just about to pack away and leave the table when Sarki brings out omelettes. The omelettes turn out to be the culinary highlight of the day.

We have a lunch of boiled mushrooms, boiled potato and boiled green beans, accompanied by tuna-and-onion sandwich. As a non-fish eater I have to confine myself to the boiled vegetables.

Then for dinner we have mashed potatoes, curried carrot and potato, and more tuna. If tuna is to be the staple then I'm going to struggle for protein.

To give Sarki his due, he's hindered by the fact that Phil doesn't like rice, and won't let him cook it. Dal bhat (rice and lentils) equals protein, but potato plus potato equals only carbohydrate.

I don't think vegetables alone will get me up the mountain.

DAY 11
INTERNET CAFÉ

Tuesday, 13 September 2011 – Manaslu Base Camp, Nepal

At last it's a clear morning, and I climb out of my tent at eight o'clock for my first view of Manaslu in nearly three years. The impressive and somewhat daunting East Pinnacle rises above us, though the rather more straightforward main summit is out of view behind it. A snow slope eases down to the North Col between the East Pinnacle and the North Peak; this will be our route of ascent if all goes well.

After breakfast I go for a short amble above base camp, where a good path meanders up a ridge of moraine in the direction of Camp 1. After 200m of ascent – my altimeter reads 5,050m – I catch up with Mark, Ian and Mila waiting beneath a short rock band where the fixed ropes begin. Robert was with them and has gone for a short scramble up the rock band, but he soon returns and we descend to base camp together.

On the way down Robert tells me about the time he took Viagra on Everest.

'Man, that's a miracle drug. I was so strong I could've just kept on going.'

'I won't ask if there were any side effects,' I reply.

He laughs. 'None – there was no third leg or extra wood. It'll get you aroused if that's what you're after, but if you're not then it just gives you more energy.'

The fine weather lasts until about one o'clock; we're able to have hot showers and dry our clothes in the sun. At lunch time the wet mist of previous days drifts across camp again, and at three o'clock, while I'm in the communications tent drafting a blog post, it really starts hammering down and everything is grey.

Two Italians dressed from head to toe in sponsor logos poke their heads in and ask if they can use the internet. We've only just been able to charge up the batteries with the sun this morning, and this is the first time any of us have had a chance to use it. They offer to pay the cost of sending a message, but we've paid a little more than this to have all the apparatus of laptops, satellite receivers, batteries and solar panels carted up the Budhi Gandaki for six days by porters. The idea that people on budget expeditions – who have brought no internet connection of their own – can barge in and treat our comms tent as an internet café, posting messages on behalf of their sponsors, irritates me. They pounce on Anne-Mari, who is sitting at the workstation next to me, and ask if they can use her SIM card. I would have told them where to go, but they probably guessed that by my twisted expression.

Anne-Mari is kinder to them. They put her under pressure, and she agrees to let them if they come back later. We discuss it collectively at dinner, and agree to send them away if they come back. They can always use the commercial internet connection at the lodge in Samagaon if they're desperate. In an emergency we would certainly let them use our satellite phones, but even the most shoestring of expedition teams should make their own provision for this.

DAY 12
TOUGH GUY IAN

Wednesday, 14 September 2011 – Manaslu Base Camp, Nepal

The climbing proper begins today, as we make our first foray up to Camp 1 to leave a load and acclimatise to the higher altitudes. We take a seven o'clock breakfast and leave in ones and twos between 7.15 and 7.45.

I depart at 7.25 with Mark, Ian and Tarke, and slowly lead the way on the clear path up the ridge of moraine we wandered up yesterday. It's slightly harder going with a pack on my back. I decide to start with a light load, taking just my sleeping bag, Therm-a-Rest and eating utensils to leave at Camp 1.

The sun is beating down; very quickly I'm sweating into my eyes and have to keep stopping to wipe them. My sunglasses steam up as the sweat evaporates. Initially I decide to walk without them, but this won't be an option when we're on the glacier and snow blindness becomes a risk.

I reach the place we halted last time, where a fixed rope leads up a short rock scramble, and stop for some water. Ian and Mark go ahead while Tarke waits. Refreshed, I move on and find the scrambling easy – the fixed rope is really just a precaution. At the top it levels off and we ascend gently along a rock band for a few hundred metres. Many streams run across and I have to take care not to slip, but otherwise it's easy ground.

We arrive at the edge of the glacier where Mark, Ian and Mila are putting on crampons. Mila complains of being slow, but if she's slow then I must be climbing in a suit of chainmail. Phil and the Sherpas excepted, the two quickest in our team are the two women, Anne-Mari and Mila. I don't know about the other guys, but I couldn't be less embarrassed if they were Reinhold Messner's twin daughters. Phil, Mila and Anne-Mari set off ahead of us; this is the last we see of them for several hours. Meanwhile, Mark, Ian, Tarke and I set off slowly in pursuit.

*Onto the Manaslu Glacier, with the
East Pinnacle and North Peak up ahead*

The glacier slants up at a comfortable angle, not too

steep, but enough to keep things interesting. We make quick progress to begin with. The ice is dry, without much surface snow. This means that crevasses are easy to spot and we're able to climb unroped. To make things easier, the Sherpas of Russell Brice's Himex team have fixed ropes across the crevasses so that we can clip in for extra safety.

After an hour the route steepens, and up ahead we can see Karel crouched in the snow. Poor chap – he has diarrhoea. It can't be much fun completing your business when you're wearing three layers and a climbing harness. Ian is leading and Steve has caught up with us. We overtake Karel to reach a steep section of ice cut in two by a narrow crevasse. As Ian stops to wait for another climber to cross, Karel catches Steve and starts prodding him in the back.

'C'mon, c'mon,' he says.

Mark and I climb halfway up the steep section to reach the edge of the crevasse, but Ian is still standing at the other end and hasn't moved. As we edge our way along the edge of the crevasse he calmly shouts across to us.

'I think I've dislocated my shoulder.'

I look at Mark, and he rolls his eyes. Neither of us say a word.

Karel pushes past me, and tries to push past Mark.

'Hang on, mate, we've got a serious injury here.'

But Karel's bowels can't wait. Ian steps back across the crevasse; Karel eases past and walks on.

The rest of us are going nowhere.

'Anyone know what to do here?' Mark says.

I shrug. 'Snap his arm off?' I'm almost tempted to reply.

Ian's right shoulder is twisted at an unnatural angle and his arm sticks out in front of him like an elephant's trunk.

'Can you pop it back in for me, please?' he says.

I see Mark wince. I imagine that my own reaction is much the same.

'I don't think you want me to do that, mate,' Mark replies.

'I have no idea how,' I tell him. 'I'm sure I'd just bugger it up further if I tried.'

We look at Steve, who is looking just as horrified at the thought.

Ian gasps in pain as we help him off with his pack. Mark gets his radio out to call Phil and ask for advice.

'Slight problem here, Phil. Ian's dislocated his shoulder.'

There is a slight pause before Phil's voice comes over the air. 'Is he down a crevasse – do you need me to come down and help?' He speaks as though this sort of thing happens all the time.

'No. No crevasse is involved. He's just dislocated his shoulder, but we don't know how to get it back in.'

'Is Tarke still with you? Ask him to take Ian back down to base camp. Himex has a team doctor who should be able to help.'

And so Ian is spared the prospect of three of us prodding around with his helpless arm like some sort of mediaeval torture.

We continue on. The trail doubles back over the crevasse and there's a small jump upwards. It's relatively easy ground, and although we need to twist slightly, we're still baffled how Ian managed to dislocate his shoulder.

'Take care!' I shout to Mark as he crosses ahead of me. 'It's normally you who gets the stupid injuries.'

I'm remembering how Mark managed to break his ankle while the two of us were coming down from Island Peak two years ago. The injury led to him abandoning the expedition to Gasherbrum that Ian, Phil and I embarked upon a few weeks later.

Beyond Dislocation Crack, as I decide to name it, the glacier flattens and the sun comes out. We can see figures climbing a steep shoulder of snow some distance ahead of us. At the top of the shoulder tents are pitched beneath a triangle of rock.

'I think that's Russell's camp,' Steve says. 'Camp 1 is a little higher.'

Himex have a huge team of climbers, some twenty or so clients and a similar number of Sherpas, so they need to camp away from everyone else. I'm glad Steve has told me this. It means that I can keep motivated beyond the tents that we see in the distance. They seem quite close now, but I've started dripping sweat into my eyes again. My glasses have steamed up like I'm in a Turkish bath, and I'm finding it difficult to see where I'm going. I have no option but to stop and clean them. I'm blinded by the bright snow when I take them off, but it has to be done. By the time I'm finished Steve and Mark are far ahead, and I follow slowly behind.

A little while later, as I ascend the snow slope beneath Russell's camp, half a dozen of our Sherpa crew come running down from a load carry up to the higher camps.

'One hour, one hour,' Gombu says to me as he passes.

Clearly I still have some way to go; at Russell's camp my altimeter only reads 5,550m. A series of snow saddles lead around the rock triangle and up behind it. At each rise I hope to see more tents, but at each one I'm disappointed. Anne-Mari and Mila are the next to pass in the other direction, having reached Camp 1. I tell them about Ian's shoulder.

'Silly, I don't know how he did it.'

'I know, but it's so easy,' Anne-Mari says. 'My husband dislocated his shoulder falling over on the patio at home.'

I expect Ian would be heartened by this story – if you're going to do it, then I guess leaping a crevasse is a more exciting way to go.

I move on and reach the top of another rise. I turn around and immediately do a double take. There are two faintly familiar figures behind me. I'm sure the second one looks like Tarke. I look again and see that I'm not deceived – it's Tarke and Ian. Did they find someone to fix Ian's shoulder? Instead of continuing down to base camp, he has picked up his pack and climbed back up. Despite his sore shoulder and my head start, he's still catching up with me – he's some guy.

At the top of the penultimate rise, the trail loops to the left to reach a plateau on top of the rock triangle behind Russell's camp. Phil is standing on top of it looking down. It takes me a long time to reach him. I'm pretty tired now. It's been a big jump in altitude today and I'm feeling the effects. The sun is hot, it's a steep climb, and every ten steps I have to pause and take a few deep breaths. It's the sort of walking I usually do on summit day.

I reach Camp 1 at midday and dump my gear in a tent that Mark has already claimed for us. Ian and Tarke are not far behind me. Ian tells me that he decided to pop his own shoulder back into place by leaning on it.

'It's still really painful,' he says.

I try to look sympathetic, in the same way you would talk to a man who's deliberately chosen to wear a floral shirt.

Mark roars with laughter.

'I'm not bloody surprised,' he says. 'I would rather clean my arse with a boat hook. Why didn't you go down and get the doctor to do it? You're a nutter.'

Phil gives Ian a dose of Tramadol, a strong painkiller, for the journey back down.

'Dude, take some of this and you won't feel a thing. You won't know who you are or what you're doing,' Phil says.

'You could also do that by offering him a drink,' Mark says.

Camp 1 is on a flat promontory looking out over the glacier we've just ascended. Mark stands a few feet away from me, looking down. He tells me he can see all the way down to base camp and beyond, but I'm too exhausted to move from my position and have a look. I slump in the tent for five minutes and gulp down some water. Then I get up, heave on a much lighter pack and head back down with Tarke and Ian.

It's slow progress. Ian is clearly still in pain despite the Tramadol, and he has to keep stopping. After about forty-five minutes of descent, just before we reach Dislocation Crack, Tarke tells me to go on ahead.

Robert shoots past me on skis. He arrived at Camp 1 much later than us but says he has taken just six minutes to descend. Beyond this he meets trickier ground, with more crevasses and loose rocks which make descending on skis hazardous. I keep catching him on foot, and there are a few sections he finds difficult without crampons. On one of these I lend him my abseil device to descend a steep slope I can walk down easily with my spikes. The snow picket holding the fixed rope is loose; I have to jam my ice axe in front of it and push so that Robert can descend in safety.

The rest of the descent is straightforward if tiring. I stagger in to base camp at 2.30 with the rest of the team right behind me. Back at camp, Ian goes to see Russell's base camp doctor, Monica. She examines his shoulder and discovers that it's still dislocated. She gets him to lie down and she clicks it back into place.

What an idiot (Ian, not Monica).

I'm dehydrated, and I find it difficult to force down my lunch. I spend the rest of the afternoon sleeping. But it's been a good day.

DAY 13
RAIN, RAIN, RAIN

Thursday, 15 September 2011 – Manaslu Base Camp, Nepal

Today is another of those horrible damp, grey and drizzly days at base camp, with occasional bursts of heavy rain. There's barely a glimmer of sun all day; I spend most of it cowering in my tent. There has been enough sun to charge the solar panels, though, and for the first time since arriving at base camp last Sunday we have internet access. Phil shows us how to use the BGAN/Inmarsat satellite connection, but he finds it all a bit frustrating. As the most IT-literate in the team I end up taking over and showing everyone how to set up their accounts and send email. I wait till the afternoon – morning back in the UK – to send out a blog post covering the trek in and our little foray up to Camp 1 yesterday. I don't mention Ian's dislocated shoulder, as things like that can worry people at home.

Although we've only just started climbing, at lunch we discuss logistics for getting out of here once the expedition is over. If we want to get a helicopter back to Kathmandu then we need to order it long before we start on our summit push, but helicopters are expensive – anything from $1,000 to $1,500 US dollars per person, depending on how many of us chip in for it, and whether we get a large military or small commercial one. The alternative is to trek out. That will involve waiting in Samagaon for three days for porters to arrive from Arughat, and then spending several days trekking back the way we came. And then there's the bumpy truck ride from Arughat, which admittedly should be easier now the monsoon is passing. It will take more than a week longer – not very appealing after an exhausting climb, but the alternative is expensive.

Mark sums up the dilemma from his point of view.

'It's going to cost us a thousand dollars in beer if we trek out,' he says.

Mark has been relatively subdued for most of the expedition so far. Often he dominates the conversation, but this time he's generally kept quiet, piping up with the occasional gem of wisdom, usually facetious.

Afterwards we discuss Anne-Mari, our Finnish teammate who is comfortably the strongest in the group despite her much lighter build. Mila tells us Anne-Mari even accused Phil, who is as strong as a Sherpa at high altitude, of going a bit slowly during our foray to Camp 1 yesterday.

'I remember seeing her on Everest,' Karel says. 'She was like a cat climbing through the icefall with her hands and feet. So quick.'

'Well, down in Samagaon a few days ago she went for a run,' I reply. 'I've never known that happen before – someone going for a run in the middle of an expedition. At high altitude.'

If Anne-Mari is lucky she'll have a chance to exercise her limbs again tomorrow. We're going to wait for Phil's weather forecast, but the plan is to go up to Camp 1 and sleep there before going to Camp 2 to sleep the following day. We can all expect headaches and (if we're lucky) vivid dreams.

DAY 14
ALPINE SQUATTING

Friday, 16 September 2011 – Camp 1, Manaslu, Nepal

It will be our first night on the mountain today. The plan is to set off after lunch when conditions are a little more overcast, so that we won't be climbing in sweltering heat. This morning is all about preparation and waiting. The food has improved a lot since our first day at base camp, when the monks were here for our puja and Sarki had a lot of work to do looking after them. The stodgy food we got that day was an exception. Today he cooks us a big breakfast.

Steve, who normally hasn't been eating that much, tucks down a mountain of food.

'Dude, how do you eat so much – where does it go?' Phil says.

'Well, if you hang around a couple of hours, I'll show you,' Steve replies.

Mila, who has been strong until now, appears to be under the weather when it matters. She skipped dinner last night, and says she's feeling ill again this morning. She seems to be nervous – I wonder how much of her illness is psychological. I try to reassure her.

'You were quicker up there than all of us last time, and it's just one foot in front of the other.'

I look round to seek reassurance from someone else, but sitting the other side of her is Ian.

'I mean, what could go wrong, Ian?'

We all start laughing. There can't be many ways of dislocating your shoulder on the easy climb up to Camp 1, but Ian managed to find one.

Ascending dry ice on the Manaslu Glacier

We set off at 12.30, straight after lunch. I should be better acclimatised this time, but still I decide to take it easy, plodding very slowly up the moraine. Halfway up I pass Mila, going much more slowly than last time. Eventually she decides to return to base camp. By the time we reach the start of the glacier and put on our crampons I find myself on my own. I remain so for most of the climb, plodding slowly on dry snow in overcast conditions.

After about three hours, just short of Russell's camp,

my throat starts getting dry and I decide to get my water bottle out and hang it off the front of my rucksack so that I can swig as I climb. The water gives me a renewed burst of energy. I overtake Mark and Karel, arriving into Camp 1 at 4.15.

A surprise awaits us. Two French climbers have used one of our tents and put a big hole in it with either an axe or crampons. Now it's unusable. Their excuse is that they couldn't tell which tent was theirs when they came down from Camp 2. This seems as likely as chocolate-coated snow. Their tent is much smaller and not as securely fastened as ours, which had all of Karel's kit in it from our load carry two days ago. It's obvious they are lying. They decided to use a better tent because it happened to be there, and they didn't expect its owners to show up and demand it back.

Phil is surprisingly generous about it.

'I don't mind them using my tents in an emergency as long as they look after them. These guys are climbing on a shoestring and I used to do that myself. It's obvious they're not mountaineers, so we need to give 'em some slack.'

I'm not so sympathetic. If they're not mountaineers, what are they doing on the mountain? Would they have used our food and fuel had they found that in the tent as well? People often arrive at camp in difficult circumstances and expect to find food, gas and certainly their tent in a usable condition. Shoestring or no shoestring, this was no emergency. The climbers had their own tent next door. There's no real excuse for their behaviour.

'Are they going to pay for the tent?' I ask.

'Will they fuck,' Phil replies.

Tarke isn't happy either. He carried the tent up here and

pitched it for us, his paying clients. Now he has to pack it up and carry it down again. He knows the French climbers will give him no tip and no thanks. Phil has to talk him out of returning the favour by putting a hole through their tent with his crampons.

It's cold when we arrive in camp. Mark and I spend the next couple of hours boiling water and rehydrating in our tent, which luckily is still in one piece. Gombu has brought up croissants and apple pie cooked by Sarki in base camp, so for once I have a tasty high-altitude meal instead of the horrible freeze-dried stuff which is usually our high camp staple. We fill our water bottles with melted snow before turning in for some sleep at seven o'clock.

DAY 15
SERACS

Saturday, 17 September 2011 – Camp 2, Manaslu, Nepal

We're supposed to be leaving at six o'clock this morning to pass through the dangerous serac section between Camps 1 and 2 before the sun gets too hot. When I wake up to daylight and look at my watch, it's 5.30 and there are no sounds from the neighbouring tents. I lean forward and light the stove to heat some water for tea. Mark and I melted lots of water for our bottles yesterday afternoon, so we're feeling reasonably well hydrated.

It's not too cold for a morning at 5,770m – +1°C inside the tent – but it's also quite wet, and I get cold fingers packing away my things. Outside the weather is beautiful, and it's my first chance to see the climb ahead of us to Camp 2. It's pleasing to the eye, up an intricate series of serac platforms, but it's also quite daunting – there appears to be no clear route through without surmounting sheer ice cliffs. Phil told us earlier that there's a steep section at the beginning, but then it slackens off. I don't know whether he said this to encourage us, or because the route was different two years ago when he was last here, but it's clearly going to be much harder than this.

Studying the maze of seracs to Camp 2 from Camp 1

I set off slowly at seven o'clock with Mark, Ian and
Gombu, a Sherpa I climbed with on Gasherbrum two years
ago. The route goes over two rounded snow lumps before
turning to the left and climbing sharply up a short snow
ramp. Then there's a long, flat traverse to the left. It's
probably the most dangerous section of the whole climb,
because it passes directly beneath a wall of seracs. But it's
also the easy bit: beyond this the real climbing starts. We
head up a section known as the Hourglass, and soon
discover why it has this name. A narrow couloir, climbers
need to wait in line to squeeze through it, like sand in an
hourglass.

We pass between two seracs to a wall of snow that's
steep enough to warrant a jumar to give extra protection
and leverage. Ahead of us an elderly Japanese woman is
struggling in front of her two Sherpas. She can take only
one or two steps before she needs to stop and rest for
several seconds.

I reach a place where I think I'm able to get past, but I will need to unclip from the rope and free climb past them with no protection except my crampons and ice axe. I look back; trusty Gombu indicates that I should give it a go. There are large steps in the snow and the climbing is straightforward, but I need to speed up in order to get past. I'm exhausted by the time I've overtaken all three of them, and I never quite recover from it.

I reach the top of the Hourglass after much puffing and panting, and collapse in a flattish area beneath the next series of seracs. I hoped the climb would flatten out after this, but above me I can see high walls of fluted ice rising every bit as vertically as the section we've just climbed. I look at my altimeter. We've climbed only 200m, less than a third of today's ascent. I steel myself for the next section of climbing, and hope it becomes gentler after the two walls of seracs I see above me.

The next part is intricate. We pass up a snow gully, traverse to the left then back again. There's a wide crevasse spanned by a five-metre aluminium ladder. I get down on all fours and pass over it, being careful to focus on the rungs without looking down into its depths. This is not the coolest way to get across, but I'm hardly going to look like Miles Davis if I fall in.

The trail continues up a 45° slope which ends in another near-vertical snow gully. I lever myself up with the help of my ice axe, and am dismayed to see yet another serac wall above me. How long will this steep climbing continue before the slope eases? I put down my pack and stop for a rest. I'm exhausted. We've still covered less than half the vertical distance to camp, and I wonder how many more of these steep seracs I can take.

Steve and Ian go on ahead while Gombu waits for me

and Mark to rest. I prepare myself for the next serac. It's hard work, and at the top I see another steep snow slope followed by a short traverse and another serac wall.

This is excruciating. I feel like I'm in a serac time warp. At the top of the slope I have to stop for another rest, and now I think about turning back. The unremitting steepness is boring me, and I know I'll be able to tackle it more easily when I'm better acclimatised. I think about descending to Camp 1 for a night and coming back up to Camp 2 on another rotation. One more serac, I say to myself, and things might ease.

I shoulder my pack and plod along the traverse. I have difficulty on the next steep section – the footsteps have eroded into soft snow, and I need to use my jumar to pull myself up by the arms. At the top I can see another huge wall of ice above me. Ian is walking along the top of it, having followed a trail to the right which leads around the back. We still have at least another 200m of ascent.

I stop for another rest.

'Does it continue like this all the way to camp?' I ask Gombu, who has been here before.

'Yes,' he replies.

'Then I think I'm going to return to Camp 1.'

'Why?'

I see a look of perplexity on his face – or is it contempt? This is *déjà vu* for him. We were climbing together on Gasherbrum I two years ago, and I was so exhausted and dehydrated that he had to stop on the glacier, unpack his stove and melt snow for me to drink before I could continue.

'Just climb up here. Soon you see Russell's camp,' he says. 'We camp just above this.'

Mark is as tired as I am, but he's determined to

continue, and I agree to follow for a little longer. He leads off this time. We pass underneath the ice wall. The trail around the back is not too bad, and soon we're walking along the crest where we saw Ian. There's a short mound of snow to walk up before a long flat traverse to the left. We cross a wide balcony of snow high above the roof of the world, and the easing of the terrain gives me a chance to appreciate my surroundings for the first time since we left Camp 1.

It's an unbelievable setting looking out over the Budhi Gandaki valley from a great height. It's the sort of view I would happily trade exhaustion for a hundred times, and I revel in it.

At the end of the balcony we cross a crevasse and see the tents of Camp 2 at the top of the slope in front of us. There are no more serac walls to climb, just an easy-angled slope, and at last I know I'll be able to reach camp.

The tents belong to Russell's team; it takes another half hour of slow plod to reach them, taking a few steps at a time followed by a rest. Here I stop to talk to a friend, Pierre, whom I climbed Aconcagua with last Christmas. It's not yet midday, and it's taken us less than five hours to get this far. Russell Brice's team have been on the mountain much longer than we have, and Pierre offers me some encouragement: it was their second ascent, when they were much better acclimatised, before he managed to do it inside five hours. Pierre's a strong climber. Despite my exhaustion I realise we've made good time.

I can see Phil standing and waving at the top of a short, steep slope above us. With the end in sight I'm able to shoot up it quickly. Phil is in good spirits. He and the superhuman Anne-Mari took just three hours to get here and have had a long rest. He points out Camp 3 at the top of a broad snow slope directly above us.

'Good work, buddy. You've done the hardest part of the climb. Above this it's just a walk.'

If he's telling the truth then it's encouraging. I'm good at walking – it's the climbing I struggle with. Phil says if we're feeling strong enough we can go up to Camp 3 this afternoon and tag it, before coming back down again. But Mark and I decide it's better to spend the afternoon rehydrating.

Our Camp 2 comprises six tents on a rib of snow. The giant slope leading up to Camp 3 poses an avalanche risk, but we're sheltered from it by a wall of seracs in front of a small snow gully. This should funnel any falling snow off to the side.

In the afternoon Gombu builds a toilet at one end of the rib – something of an architectural masterpiece. Behind a wall of snow he builds some steps leading down to a small ledge. Beneath this he digs another pit to crap into. It's sheltered and private, and since ours are the only tents up here, we have it to ourselves.

I have a good snooze and write up my diary, but we spend most of the time melting snow on the stove, and by the end of the afternoon we feel well hydrated. Mark is even able to eat some rice and chicken, but I know I can afford to starve myself tonight, since we'll be back in base camp tomorrow.

DAY 16
ABOVE THE CLOUDS

Sunday, 18 September 2011 – Manaslu Base Camp, Nepal

I have a restless night plagued by a headache, but all things considered I get plenty of sleep. Others don't fare so well. In the middle of the night I hear Robert retching in the tent next to us, and Robin is sick three times. In the morning we discover Steve was caught short during the night and, unable to make it to Gombu's luxury toilet, he crapped outside his tent. Phil gives him some stick about it.

'Dude, that's not cool – there's a toilet over there. Take your shit over to it, but don't use the snow shovel – we need it to make drinking water.'

Steve is apologetic and obedient.

I get cold fingers putting my crampons on, and can't tighten them much because the straps are frozen. But it's actually quite mild for 6,400m. Nobody feels like going up to Camp 3 to tag it, not even Anne-Mari. At seven o'clock we begin descending. I leave with Ian and Mark. Ian is usually much quicker than we are, but he hasn't slept well either.

'I don't think I've ever had a worse night on a

mountain,' he says.

Mark disappears ahead of us, but Ian is content to walk behind me. The seracs don't seem as steep on the way down. There is no need to abseil, and mostly we're able to descend by means of an arm wrap, facing out and coiling the fixed rope around an arm for security. When I get to the ladder over a crevasse, I cross it crabwise, facing upwards on all fours – it's not very elegant and I feel like a novice breakdancer, but it's effective and safe.

Mark is waiting above the Hourglass and we have a short rest. This steeper section is true to its name again. Many climbers are coming up and I have to keep unclipping from the rope to let them past, then planting my axe and crampons into the slope as I wait. It's slow and painful but much safer than descending unroped.

Among seracs above Camp 1, with the East Pinnacle above

I'm tired when we stagger in to Camp 1 at nine o'clock. Ian says he's been careful because he's nervous about his shoulder popping out again, a trick he doesn't want to repeat. We stay at Camp 1 for just ten minutes to dump kit we don't need lower down, such as sleeping bags, mat and helmet. The sun came out briefly during the descent from Camp 2, but we complete the journey from Camp 1 to base camp in thick cloud and light snow. It's a strange world of black and white; only the figures of Mark and Ian ahead provide a splash of colour. By the time we reach the end of the glacier and remove our crampons, the snow has turned to rain.

As we cross the band of rock we see Mila coming up the other way with one of our Sherpas, Pasang Ongchu. Mila's feeling a little better, and is going up to Camp 1 to get back on the same acclimatisation schedule as the rest of us. I don't envy her ascending in this weather.

Our descent of the moraine ridge to base camp drags on. Mark, Ian, Robert and I stagger in together at eleven o'clock. We're back in a land of grey mist and persistent rain which continues for the rest of the day, but it's good to be back here. Our time above Camp 1 provided us with our only 24-hour period free of snow or rain since arriving here. It's encouraging to know the weather seems to be better higher up. This is because we are climbing above the clouds.

I spend the day catching up with the sleeping and eating I missed out on up the mountain. Steve has to put up with endless jokes about 'going to the bathroom' outside his tent.

'There may be three or four inches of snow up there, but not the heavy dumping that was predicted,' Phil says as we discuss the weather forecast.

'There was some heavy dumping outside Steve's tent, though,' someone replies.

Later in the evening Steve is curious why everyone finds it so hard to sleep at the higher camps.

'What's the reason for this – is it just because of the lower oxygen levels, or is there something else?' he asks.

'It depends,' Phil says. 'If someone's sharing a tent with you then it's obvious why they don't get any sleep.'

We roar with laughter.

DAY 17
BANTER

Monday, 19 September 2011 – Manaslu Base Camp, Nepal

Today is the worst day yet at base camp. It rains heavily all day without respite. Both the comms tent and dining tent leak, and we have bowls in each of them catching water drops. At breakfast we discuss the latest weather forecast. It's relatively benign, with low wind speeds and not much snow – high winds and snow are the two things that will stop us climbing the mountain. It's strange, because there's been a huge amount of precipitation at base camp, but it's all fallen as rain and hasn't translated to snow higher up the mountain.

There's some confusion about measurements. Americans always describe altitude in feet, while the rest of us talk in metres. Our forecasts give snow levels in inches, which we Brits understand, but I have to convert them into centimetres for the benefit of Anne-Mari, a Finn.

We get talking about jobs.

'In my job I always talk in point sizes and pixels,' I say, 'which is exactly the same as Mark, who's pixelated most of the time.'

Nobody laughs, and it seems like tumbleweed is

blowing across the table.

'Was that a joke?' Phil says.

'It's hard to tell,' Mark replies. 'I think it's what in the UK we call a "shit joke".' He gestures a pair of quotation marks in the air with his fingers.

Halfway through the morning Mila and Pasang Ongchu call us on the radio from Camp 2 after taking just three and a half hours to ascend there from Camp 1. Mila has been strong all along, but even so I'm amazed – this is nearly as quick as Phil and Anne-Mari two days ago.

'She's only twenty-four,' Phil says. 'When I was twenty-four I used to take only ten seconds…' He pauses for a few moments, '…But let's talk about my climbing instead.'

Phil's jokes are worse than mine. It doesn't get any better at afternoon tea. There is news of an earthquake in Sikkim, across Nepal's eastern border with India. We learn that it claimed four casualties in Kathmandu after a wall collapsed. Some of the team have received emails from concerned friends and family. Two members of the team felt the earthquake in base camp last night, but most of us didn't.

Robin is one of the ones who did.

'You needed to be sitting in a chair,' he says. 'If you were lying on your back in the tent then you would have felt nothing.'

'Is that what your wife said?' Phil asks.

We laugh.

DAY 18
GROUNDHOG DAY

Tuesday, 20 September 2011 – Manaslu Base Camp, Nepal

It's getting a bit like Groundhog Day here at base camp, except that I wake up to the relentless pounding of rain on the roof of my tent, rather than Sonny and Cher singing *I Got You Babe*. It's usually around 6.30, and I lie inside my sleeping bag for an hour or so, sometimes reading a chapter or two of my book, before getting up to join the rest of the team for eight o'clock breakfast in the dining tent. Every morning is the same. There's a grey mist in the air, and I can barely see the wall of frozen ice blocks above Russell Brice's camp just a few short metres away. I never see any of the mountain above, which is always hidden from view behind clouds. A toilet tent rises by the side of the trail about twenty metres above our camp; usually that's the limit of my vision.

The rain continues all day, with a couple of half-hour windows when it stops and voices can be heard outside.

'It's clearing!'

'Yes, it's definitely improving!'

But it never does. I can't think of anywhere I've been where it's rained so much, for so long, every day. Had we arrived at the start of the month, like Russell's team, then we would have suffered three whole weeks of it. As it is, this is only our ninth day here. The good news is that this dismal weather seems to be confined to a narrow band of altitude which just happens to coincide with our base camp. Everyone who's been above Camp 1 – including us – has reported clear weather, and there's actually been very little snowfall higher up the mountain. This means it's much safer than usual, and I'd happily sacrifice good weather at base camp for a safe summit window. If that happens then it can rain every day here for all I care.

Mila came down from Camp 2 yesterday, and at breakfast she's concerned because Phil has received an email from her sister. She's not at all happy about it. Apparently her sister isn't supposed to know she's on the mountain, and if her sister knows then it won't be long before her father will know, and that's a big problem.

'There's definitely a story here,' I remark, 'and at some point you're going to have to tell us what it is.'

'Yeah, what's your dad going to do if he finds out?' Mark says.

'What *won't* he do?' Mila replies.

'Well, I asked first,' Mark says, 'and since I don't know the guy and you do, I think it's only fair you answer first.'

At which point Mila loses the thread of the conversation in a confusion of logic.

Eventually the panic is over when she reads the offending email herself and realises it's not from her sister at all, but her mother pretending to be her sister. This is apparently much less concerning. It also has the effect of shielding her from further interrogation as Mark and I conclude the whole family must be bonkers.

Having caught up with my diary the previous day and

sent out a blog post, I spend today alternately reading and snoozing. I even have a shower to help pass the time. Mark, Ian and I decide we can't stew here in base camp any longer and must go out. We agree to descend to Samagaon tomorrow, though there's a strong chance our motivation for this scheme will evaporate when confronted with the same horrible weather.

DAY 19
BEER IN SAMAGAON

Wednesday, 21 September 2011 – Manaslu Base Camp, Nepal

A change, at least to begin with. When I wake up this morning there's no sound of rain pattering on my tent. I even have hopes the sky will be clear. But when I look out of my tent it's so misty I can barely see Phil's tent six feet away from mine. It's not long before it starts raining again.

Despite the bad weather, we keep our resolution to go down to Samagaon for some exercise. Ian, Mark, Anne-Mari and Karel leave straight after breakfast, but I have a spot of tent difficulty I need to sort out before I go. There are no obvious leaks, but every morning there's a patch of dampness on the carpet inside my tent – if I leave anything lying there it becomes saturated with moisture. By morning this means a part of my sleeping bag is wet, and there are some clothes I've been unable to get dry because they keep ending up there. It's as if my tent is pitched in a pool of water that keeps soaking through. At breakfast Mark tells me he had the same problem, and discovered it was because water was collecting in pools on the tarpaulin underneath his groundsheet. He fixed it by emptying the tarpaulin and folding the edges underneath the tent so that it didn't collect any more rainwater.

It's likely my problem is the same, but emptying the tarpaulin is easier said than done. I struggle for several minutes, lying prostrate on the moraine as I try to spoon water out with a rock. Luckily Sarki notices and brings one of his kitchen crew over to help. Between us we lift the whole tent up and shift it a few feet away, allowing us to pull out the tarpaulin and empty it. I hope this will fix the problem, but it takes about an hour, and it's ten o'clock by the time I leave for Samagaon in thick mist.

I have the foresight to unpack my walking stick before I set off, and it comes in handy. It's relaxing descending the moraine ridge immediately below camp; the terrain is firm and the ground falls away steeply to my left, leaving behind a fast-flowing cascade of water far below. I cross a stream at the end of this section and everything changes. It's raining heavily now and I'm into the vegetation zone. There are many porters coming up, and the trail is extremely muddy, much more than when we came up over a week ago. The lower I get the worse it becomes, a quagmire of slippery filth, and but for my stick I would be falling on my backside time after time.

The trail is surprisingly busy. As well as the porters, I pass Mingma, a climbing Sherpa I climbed Chulu Far East with three years ago, on his way up with a single Indian client. One of our kitchen crew, Wongchu, passes me with some more supplies; a group of somewhat clueless but friendly French climbers stop me for a chat; and an American who looks like the actor Jim Carrey passes me near the bottom. He tells me it's taken him three and a half hours to get that far and he's 'budgeted' six. I suspect he may need to re-budget, but he seems cheerful enough. As I approach Samagaon I pass Karel on his way back up again.

He was unable to recharge his camera batteries in the teahouse and doesn't seem to be in a good mood.

'With no electricity, there is no reason to go there,' he says.

But one reason is Tuborg beer, and I continue. I arrive at the teahouse at midday. Mark, Ian and Anne-Mari tell me they were about to leave, but when they saw me through the window arriving along the trail, they ordered another round and sat down again. Anne-Mari is disappointed because it's too muddy in Samagaon to go for the run she had been hoping for. She had the consolation of sitting in a teahouse watching Mark and Ian drink instead, a less healthy but arguably more entertaining alternative.

I stay and chat for two hours and eat a plate of deep-fried momos, but I was wet and muddy when I arrived and the teahouse isn't warm enough to get dry. By two o'clock I'm shivering, and I realise it's time to go back up to base camp. It took me four and a half hours to ascend the first time around, and it gets dark at 6.30 – I don't have long if I want to get back in daylight.

True to form, Mark and Ian are unconcerned and order another beer. They even take the precaution of borrowing Anne-Mari's head torch, so I don't expect to see them again tonight. Some of our Sherpa crew are also down at the teahouse today. I think Mark and Ian will drink all afternoon before asking for some blankets and settling down for the night here.

I return in thick mist, but at least it's no longer raining, and the muddy path has dried since this morning. I don't see another soul until Anne-Mari catches up with me on the moraine ridge close to the top. I walk slowly into camp at 5.30. It's been good exercise, but I'm cold and wet and glad to warm myself up with a dinner of pakoras and yak steak.

Ian has left his camera on the table, and I can't resist the temptation of taking a few silly photographs of bits of food arranged provocatively. It will be a nice surprise for him to discover when he looks at them after returning home from the expedition. However, I resist the old schoolboy trick of sticking his toothbrush up my arse and photographing that too.

I'm settling down into my tent when I hear Mark's voice echoing noisily across camp. He and Ian arrive back at 8.30 and must have completed most of the ascent in pitch blackness. One day the demon booze will be their downfall.

DAY 20
PREPARATIONS

Thursday, 22 September 2011 – Manaslu Base Camp, Nepal

It's a busy day. At 7.30 I'm pulled out of my sleeping bag (figuratively, not literally) to attend a pre-breakfast team meeting. Phil has some good news for us to begin with: he's secured a deal on helicopters to get us out of base camp at the end of the expedition, which means we won't have to trek back out the way we came.

So that's good; we can get off this mountain more easily at the end. But how about climbing it?

I have mixed feelings about the second piece of news: we'll be setting off on our summit push tomorrow after only four days' rest at base camp. Apart from the risk of a storm on the 24th, which we have scant information about, there seems to be a decent summit window on the 27th and 28th, without much precipitation and only slight winds.

The downside is that our acclimatisation schedule has been somewhat aggressive. In fact, to me it seems rushed. It's impossible to believe that all of us are fully – or even adequately – acclimatised, and the likelihood is that although some of us may reach the summit, others will be ill and will have to descend. I can only keep my fingers crossed I'll be in the first group. I know Robin, who was ill at Camp 2 last time, is worried. Psychological factors play a big part in altitude sickness; worry often leads to illness higher up the mountain. As for Mila, who has only spent one night sleeping on the mountain at Camp 1, it's hard to believe she'll be ready for the summit.

Whether I'm ill or not, I know it will be hard work if I'm still acclimatising. Since confidence is important I know I have to thrust this from my mind and focus on the positives. I've been to Camp 2 already: it wasn't too bad, and it will be easier next time. After that, there are two reasonably short days to Camps 3 and 4, with plenty of rehydration and recovery time. Summit day is only 750m of ascent, the same as my summit day on Muztag Ata in China, in 2007, when I climbed above 7,500m. This time I will be using oxygen. It's going to be tough, but it's nothing for me to fear.

I spend the rest of the morning preparing. Phil demonstrates the oxygen apparatus after breakfast, and with his help I spend an hour or so perfecting my harness and jumar system. Although my current rig has been adequate on several mountains, I have found both the jumar and safety carabiner cords quite short. This has led to me fighting the fixed rope as I climb – particularly when somebody else is attached below me and providing tension.

The safety system seems elaborate, but it's fairly straightforward once you get used to it. Two short lengths of cord are attached to your harness, one containing the jumar and the other containing the safety carabiner. The jumar has a catch that enables it to slide up the rope, but not down it. If you fall, the jumar locks onto the rope, holding you in place. The safety carabiner is the back-up for the moments when your jumar isn't attached to the rope. The carabiner is essentially just a ring of metal. It won't hold you in place like the jumar, but it will stop you falling any further than the end of the rope, where it's anchored to the mountain.

There is an optimum length for the cord so that you can reach the jumar or carabiner comfortably in the event of a fall. If it's too long then you won't be able to reach unless you climb back up. If it's too short then there are times when you have to stoop as you climb. Phil helps me to adjust my two bits of cord to just the right length.

I have a few other bits and pieces to do in the morning. It's the first rainless day we've had at base camp, with brief spells of sunshine. This means I'm able to dry things that have been wet for days. I take the opportunity to get some video footage of our comfortable base camp set-up, and have a pre-summit shave.

We're eating well now that chickens and yak meat have been delivered to Samagaon by helicopter. Sarki's cooking is excellent – only on puja day was the quality lacking. This aberration was because he was busy preparing food for the monks, who took priority (it goes without saying that the mountain gods are more important than climbers).

Phil is busy all day getting things ready for departure, and he seems a little distracted at dinner – not his usual gallery-playing self. We end up talking about the Italian climbers camped a short way from us at base camp.

'One of them has climbed sixteen 8,000m peaks,' Phil says.

We all know there are only fourteen 8,000m peaks.

'Sixteen? Wow, that's really good. Two of them must have been on the Moon.'

'Very funny,' Phil replies. 'He climbed a couple of them twice. Fourteen plus two makes sixteen. Do you understand?'

'We hear you clucking, big chicken,' Robert says.

But this only makes things worse, and we roar with laughter.

Meanwhile we hear the story of Mark and Ian's escape from Samagaon yesterday. At 4.30, one of the Sherpas had been sober enough to realise only two hours of daylight remained and two of Phil's clients were still drinking. Three Sherpas escorted the hapless duo back up to base camp. They completed most of the journey in darkness with just one torch between them. Our sirdar Dorje led the way, but the hardest job was given to Kami and Gombu, who had to walk at the back, ready to catch a human-sized snowball should it fall on them. I don't know if anyone can remember the TV series *It's a Knockout*, but it sounds like another episode was enacted last night.

DAY 21
CHONGBA

Friday, 23 September 2011 – Camp 1, Manaslu, Nepal

I don't have too much to do this morning. I pack the few remaining things I haven't taken up to Camp 1 already, including an extra pair of mitts, warm socks for summit day, and food for six days on the mountain. My bag feels light this time around, and floats on my back like a soft cushion.

First thing in the morning, before breakfast, we're formally introduced to our Sherpa team. I know most of them already: our sirdar Dorje has been ever present, Tarke and Gombu I know from Gasherbrum two years ago, and others like Kami and Sangye were with us on the trek in. One I don't know is Chongba. He's an important Sherpa because he will be climbing with me, carrying my spare oxygen bottle on summit day and monitoring the one I'll be using to see when it needs changing. Phil had described him to me as 'the one with no neck, like Tarke', but that wasn't much to go on.

We stand around in a circle as each of us is introduced to our respective Sherpa. When I call out Chongba's name a cheerful older man steps forward, radiating warmth, and we shake hands. I'm pleased. All the Sherpas are strong, but I prefer the older guys like Tarke and Gombu, who are wise as well as tough – an essential quality on big mountains.

Later in the morning my French friend Pierre comes over and we have tea in the dining tent. I summited Aconcagua with him a few months ago. He's climbing with Russell's team on Manaslu. He will also be leaving on his summit push this afternoon. He has been here longer than we have and has made several forays up the mountain, so he should be much stronger.

Russell Brice's team is the biggest on the mountain this year; they've been taking the lead with the rope fixing, and many other teams have been following them closely. The twenty-two clients on their team will be climbing in two waves. Eleven left yesterday, and eleven, including Pierre, leave today. Significantly, this later eleven – who will be climbing on the same schedule as we are – include the elderly Japanese climbers, who may or may not prove to be a problem for us.

The rest of our team gradually arrive in the dining tent, and I introduce some of them to Pierre. Last of all comes Phil, who is still smarting from the incident when French climbers stole our tent at Camp 1.

'You're not French, are you?' he asks Pierre.

Pierre smiles and nods politely. Phil walks to the far end of the tent to sit at the head of the table, where he barks one-liners at people like some modern-day mediaeval king in his kangaroo court. This image is enhanced by the comical King Charles I haircut he sports. I'm not entirely sure what Pierre makes of it all. Luckily he's lived in Britain for a long time; he's used to our irreverent sense of humour and seems to take it all in his stride.

We're blessed with clear weather in the morning, but at eleven o'clock it starts raining stair-rods again. We were intending to leave straight after lunch, but the rain continues and some people talk of delaying their departure until the weather has improved. When it starts raining at base camp, though, it usually sets in for the day, so I keep to my plans and leave at 12.30 with Ian and Mila. Both are speedsters, much faster than I am, but today they seem content to let me lead all the way to Camp 1. I plod like a tortoise, in no hurry to get there. The trick at high altitude is to conserve as much energy as possible until summit day.

The weather doesn't improve much. The rain turns to sleet, and then snow higher up, but throughout the afternoon it continues to fall in whatever form.

We reach Camp 1 shortly after four o'clock. There's about a foot of snow surrounding the tents, but otherwise our camp is in good condition. We get working with the spades to dig it out; most of the others arrive soon after, including my tent mate Mark. We spend the remainder of the afternoon boiling water and rehydrating. As evening approaches the snow continues, and we overhear Steve getting depressed in the next tent along from us. It's his second attempt on Manaslu, and the snow has been a feature of both expeditions.

'I'm concerned about this weather,' he says. 'Much more snow and we won't be able to go up.'

Phil is less worried, and his opinion is the one that matters. As long as the snow peters out and it's clear by the morning – as it was last time we were here – then our summit attempt can go on.

There are other things for us to consider, too. We risk suffocating inside our tents if the snow continues to fall all night and piles up outside. We're careful to ensure ventilation at roof level in both the inner and outer tents, so that several feet of snow can fall before it becomes a serious concern.

DAY 22
BEATING A RETREAT

Saturday, 24 September 2011 – Manaslu Base Camp, Nepal

I sleep well and hear no more pattering on the roof during the night. When I sit up to light the stove at six o'clock, I discover why. I push up the ceiling to dislodge any snow that may have accumulated overnight. It's heavy like a stone – there is so much snow on top that it's been muffling the sound of precipitation. As soon as the roof is clear the familiar pitter-patter begins again.

We can now hear many avalanches behind us. If they are not falling on the route up to Camp 2 then they must be close to it. Outside the tent, Camp 1 is like the Twilight Zone. There has been at least two feet of snow and most of the tents are well on the way to getting buried. One is so overloaded with the weight that Phil watches it collapse before his eyes. If we weren't here to rescue ours, they would be in danger of falling too. Dorje and Gombu are busy with shovels digging them out.

The serac walls barring the route to Camp 2 are barely visible in the whiteout, though they're only a short distance away. We have no option but to descend to base camp and wait for a better weather window.

We leave as a group because the trail is likely to be buried, and we don't want to risk anyone wandering into a crevasse. The first section down to Russell's camp poses the most danger from avalanches. We spread out to reduce the chances of triggering one.

Phil pauses at the lower camp to discuss the weather with one of Russell's team members. They tell him they're waiting in camp, but have lost contact with the rest of their team at Camp 2. Manaslu is loaded with avalanche risk above Camp 2; so much snow has fallen that it will take days to consolidate. The best place to wait is at base camp, but they are running out of time, and perhaps they've chosen to wait on the mountain instead. It doesn't seem like a good decision.

We continue our descent with Gombu leading. He does a great job of locating the trail in the fresh snow and sticking to it. Crevasses have become hidden; I fall waist deep into two of them by following behind the lighter Anne-Mari and Mila, who manage to walk across snow bridges without falling in. I'm much heavier, and feel like a lumbering idiot as I follow in their footsteps and the bridges collapse. Luckily I'm clipped to a fixed rope on both occasions, and the piles of fresh snow cushion my fall long before I need its security. I'm able to climb out by myself and continue, none the worse for my adventure bar some abuse from Mark. He is annoyed that I manage to climb out before he has time to take a photo.

The depth of snow has transformed the tricky rock scramble below the start of the glacier into a straightforward snow descent, and we're able to walk all the way to base camp without removing our crampons. It's still snowing when we arrive back at 10.15. We have suffered no harm from our two-day foray. As long as the snow consolidates and there's another weather window, we may even be better off for it. Our acclimatisation schedule was aggressive, but with another night on the mountain under our belts and some more time at base camp, we should be much stronger next time we go up.

It continues to snow at base camp all day. We become increasingly concerned about Russell's Himex climbers, who are still up on the mountain. Some are at Camp 2, which must be a treacherous place in this weather. They have avalanche slopes above and the disappearing serac maze barring their retreat below.

At seven o'clock, as we're heading to the dining tent for dinner, I see head torches weaving down the snow-clad moraine ridge above us. One by one, figures shamble into camp. It was obvious the snow would continue all day, so why did they delay their departure until they had to descend in the dark? We don't know, but the important thing is that everyone is safely off the mountain without mishap.

DAY 23
STORM AND SUMMIT STRATEGY

Sunday, 25 September 2011 – Manaslu Base Camp, Nepal

I wake in the middle of the night to the sound of pounding on my tent. It's our Sherpas and kitchen crew. They are going around camp, clearing snow so that we don't get buried while we sleep. Phil's tent is a couple of metres away from mine, and through my ear plugs I overhear him talking to Dorje.

'I've got another weather update from Michael.[1] Apparently it's going to continue all tomorrow.'

I look at my watch and see that it's two o'clock – those guys never seem to sleep. At breakfast most of the talk is about the storm. Everyone is safely back in base camp, but there's a rumour that an elderly Japanese man has broken his arm and will be evacuated by helicopter. We also learn that two more Himex climbers have had enough and do not intend to continue their climb.

We hear avalanches going off all around us. One is so loud it draws us out of the dining tent and falls continuously for five minutes. It's the longest avalanche I

---

1. Michael Fagin of West Coast Weather, our expedition weather forecaster based in Seattle.

can remember, and we see it through the mists above us, spilling down in a cascade of snow.

We learn that this region of the Himalayas is getting battered. A Buddha Air sightseeing flight has gone down somewhere near Kathmandu with eighteen dead. Phil tells me Cho Oyu is right in the path of the storm. I think of Matt Parkes, an expedition leader with Jagged Globe, whom I was on Cho Oyu with last year. On that occasion, there was so much snow that hardly anyone climbed the mountain at all. Matt is leading an expedition to Cho Oyu again this year, and must be feeling a sense of *déjà vu*.

On a lighter note, someone has built a snowman outside the kitchen tent. They have crowned it with a bobble hat, but when someone takes the hat off, Phil says that it looks like me (by which he means that it's bald). After breakfast, in Phil's absence, we discuss how to give the snowman a King Charles I floppy haircut so that it resembles Phil instead. I suggest that we take some dark hair off the heads of José and Karel, our two most hirsute team members, but neither is prepared to make the necessary sacrifice. Then Steve suggests that the best material would be yak hair. But to find a yak we would need to make a trip down to Samagaon, where Mark and Ian are likely to be distracted by Tuborg beer in the teahouse.

'That's a shame – I think a yak would be perfect,' Mark says. 'I like the idea that Phil's ridiculous haircut looks like hair from a yak's arse.'

This makes everyone around the table giggle for the next sixty seconds.

Later we discuss summit strategy – in particular, whether to sleep at each of the four high camps in sequence and summit on the fifth day, or skip a camp to reduce the number of days to four.

Anne-Mari is keen to climb from base camp straight to Camp 2, and Robert is wavering. But I'm not convinced that skipping camps provides any benefit. The overriding priority of the summit push is to take it as easy as possible until summit day. By setting off early in the morning and walking for just three or four hours, you can arrive in camp by midday and take it easy for the rest of the afternoon. You can snooze for a bit, you have plenty of time to boil water to rehydrate, you get warm, you can force down some food, perform your ablutions and turn in for an early night.

But by doubling up the days, you end up climbing through the afternoon, sometimes in the heat of the afternoon sun. You arrive in camp at perhaps four o'clock, shattered, dehydrated, and soaking with sweat. With the sun past its peak and no longer warming the tent, you're soon cold, and rushing to boil enough water to rehydrate. All your things are wet. Perhaps you end up drifting off to sleep before you're fully hydrated, and then get up dehydrated the following morning to repeat the process. A comfortable ascent becomes an exercise in endurance.

I witnessed three examples of this doubling up of camps on Gasherbrum two years ago. In all three instances it was clear the people doubling up were worse off than those who took an extra day. On the third occasion our team arrived at Camp 2 on Gasherbrum I so exhausted that we needed a full rest day to recover. This defeated the object of passing two camps in a single climb.

Karel points out that a frequently cited example of this doubling up of camps occurs on the south side of Everest. There people climb directly to Camp 2 from base camp on their summit push. But at Camp 2 on Everest there are rudimentary base camp facilities, and climbers rest for the following day in relative comfort. We have no such thing here on Manaslu. I have no intention of doubling up on my summit push; and it seems that most of the others agree.

DAY 24
BOREDOM

Monday, 26 September 2011 – Manaslu Base Camp, Nepal

We have another team meeting this morning. Phil reports that the weather forecast for the next few days is 'a bit shit'. It's not raining, but the fog around camp is like a thick industrial 1950s London pea souper (not that I ever experienced 1950s London, but it's how I imagine it must have been). The snow has set in and hardened, and it's definitely a few degrees colder now.

Phil tells us that most of Camp 2 is completely buried under snow. This has forced some of the smaller teams, who have had equipment destroyed, to abandon their expeditions. He says that Russell Brice's Himex team have written off their tents and equipment pitched at Camps 3 and 4, and several more of their members have decided to head home.

I take this information with a pinch of salt – Phil has a tendency to raise morale by painting things in the best light for our team. If all of this is true then it means we're in the best shape of anyone. We collapsed the tents at Camp 2 when we left. Although they will be buried under snow, they should be recoverable. Our Sherpas returned to

Camp 1 yesterday to dig our tents out there as well.

The forecast is for more snow and high winds, so it's likely we'll be here in base camp for a few days, but we still have plenty of time. Boredom begins to set in for the first time. I see Phil slice the head off the snowman with a shovel, and Sarki builds it up again to resemble a chess piece. I sent off a blog post yesterday, so I don't have anything more to report. Phil's wife Trish emailed my post back to him, and he's taken umbrage at my use of the phrase 'curiously coiffured expedition leader'.

Ian and I are thinking of going down to Samagaon again to relieve the boredom, but Mark insists he's going to stay put in base camp.

'It'll be strange drinking beer down in Samagaon knowing that Mark's up here sipping tea,' I say to Ian.

I can sense Mark's beard twitching next to me and feel sure he will change his mind. In the meantime Phil wants me to go over and see my friend Pierre so that I can spy on the Himex team for him. But I'm not really a base camp networker like he is.

We're going to need patience for the next few days. At least I still have plenty of books to read.

DAY 25
ANOTHER NICE MESS

Tuesday, 27 September 2011 – Manaslu Base Camp, Nepal

Another rest day, and time for some more exercise. Ian, Robin and I leave for Samagaon at 9.30. It's overcast and snowing at base camp as usual, but soon we're beneath the clouds and looking 1,400m down on the lush valley beneath us. We descend the moraine ridge to the vegetation zone, where a trail snakes through grassy moorland and a grey glacier tongue hangs down the hillside to our right. As well as armies of porters tramping up to base camp and down again, quite a few animals have trodden this trail, and there's a herd of dzos (half yak, half cow) grazing high up on the hillside. This has turned the path into a mud bath. The risk of sliding on my backside is high.

A couple of steep mountain streams crash down from our left, and we cross over them on makeshift stone bridges. The muddiest part is below the moorland zone, where the vegetation thickens as the trail weaves through knee-high clumps of juniper and dwarf rhododendron. A herder's stone cottage has been erected here and we have to wade through an unpleasant quagmire of mud. A half-hour descent through woodland brings us to the cobbled river valley – the top end of our old friend the Budhi Gandaki, which we trekked up for six days at the beginning of our expedition. From here a short and shockingly muddy trail along the flat brings us to the teahouse at Samagaon.

We arrive at 11.30 after two hours of walking. It's cold and wet, and a thick mist obscures the view up to Manaslu, as it always has. It's later in the season now; a couple of trekking groups are staying at the teahouse. We talk to an Australian and an American on their way over the Larkye La, and onward to the hidden valleys of Naar and Phu the other side of the Himalayan divide. They have an amazing trek ahead of them, which I had the good fortune of completing a few years ago, but they're disappointed not to see Manaslu. I tell them I had my first view of the main summit only this morning on the way down, when the clouds cleared briefly to reveal the East Pinnacle and the true summit peeping out beyond its left shoulder.

Two hours in the teahouse and a couple of San Miguel beers are enough for us. Before we begin the slow climb back, Ian loads up with the supplies he's been asked to take back for other members of our team. This includes six tins of Tuborg for Mark and Phil, six bottles of Sprite for Robert and Steve, and two tins of Red Bull for Mila. He even decides to buy four big bottles of San Miguel for our Sherpas. There's a good reason why I didn't agree to buy supplies for anyone – I didn't want to feel like a high-altitude porter on the climb back up to base camp – but Ian is too much of a nice guy to refuse.

We leave shortly before two o'clock. Once again the others decline my offer to let them go ahead, but this time my high-altitude tortoise pace is too quick for Ian. Every so often I look back and see him dropping behind, his booze-laden pack draped over a single shoulder to protect the one he injured. Robin and I offer to share some of the load, but he refuses. This is the man who wouldn't even let anyone carry his pack for him when his shoulder was dislocated. I slow my pace so that he can keep up.

We enter clouds again on the main ridge just below base camp, and a light snow begins blowing into our faces. We reach camp shortly after five.

Phil thinks there may be news about the summit push. Russell has invited him to a meeting of guides to discuss summit strategy. While we were on our way down to Samagaon, we saw about twenty of the Himex Sherpas returning up to base camp.

We eagerly anticipate the news when Phil returns from the Himex camp at seven o'clock.

'Man, they were shit-canned,' he tells us, then looks at me. 'I think you would say "wankered". I turned up expecting to talk about rope fixing and weather forecasts, but they'd had so much to drink they could hardly talk. None of them were making any sense, and their doctor had a potty mouth.'

'A what?' someone asks.

'A potty mouth – every other word she said was "fucking".'

'Ah, you mean she was issuing a cascade of obscenities,' Steve says rather more eloquently.

Phil continues. 'They gave me some whisky, but I don't even like whisky. I had to pretend to drink it then tip it on the floor. I don't know how long they'd been drinking for, but I had some catching up to do if they were going to make any sense. I felt a bit uncomfortable. It was embarrassing.'

Later on we have some nonsense of our own in the Altitude Junkies tent. My two old drinking buddies Mark and Ian keep passing bowls around the table until they end up with none for themselves. Mark keeps blaming Ian, but Ian seems exasperated. It's all a bit comical. Suddenly, something occurs to me that I've never noticed before. I realise that their relative statures and talkativeness bear a striking resemblance to a more famous double act.

'It's Laurel and Hardy!' I cry, creasing with laughter. 'Another nice mess you've got him into, Ian,' I try to say, but I find it hard to complete the sentence as I wipe away tears. Mark and Ian look bemused. I'm still chuckling to myself when I head to my tent for the night.

DAY 26
DA PASANG THE SUPER SUB

Wednesday, 28 September 2011 – Manaslu Base Camp, Nepal

I'm summoned from my tent before breakfast again, for another team meeting. The sky is clear for only the second morning since we arrived here, and Manaslu's East Pinnacle and North Peak rise above camp amid a sea of blue sky. It looks benign up there, but there's been so much snow over the last few days that the slopes are loaded. The snow presents an avalanche hazard, and there are strong winds higher up.

There's a rumour that an Italian team is going up today, but it's too soon after the storm. Phil hears that everyone is quitting Cho Oyu. If this is true then it will be the second successive autumn season that no one has reached the summit. It's supposed to be the easiest of the 8,000m peaks. I made an abortive attempt on Cho Oyu myself last year and know how they must feel. But here on Manaslu, we have one last summit window. Once the snow has consolidated, and before the jet-stream winds arrive on the 6th, we have an opportunity. We're aiming for an October 5th summit day, which gives us two more rest days before the big effort.

Our sirdar Dorje has left the expedition to lead a trek for a Canadian who sponsors his son's education. We will miss him, but we still have the same number of climbing Sherpas; one of the kitchen assistants, Da Pasang, has climbed Everest and is ready to step in.

Yes, that's right – in case you misheard, I'll say it again. One of the kitchen assistants, Da Pasang, has climbed Everest. We have a multi-talented team here. Not only can he cook a mean pancake, but he's carried heavy loads up the highest mountain on Earth. Talk about super subs.

DAY 27
SLEEPLESS NIGHT

Thursday, 29 September 2011 – Manaslu Base Camp, Nepal

I lie awake for a couple of hours during the night, worrying about our summit push. It seemed like a decent summit window when Phil first explained the plan yesterday, but something wasn't quite right. For much of the night this something nags at my mind, keeping me from sleep. Phil said that if October 5th is to be our summit day then we have to be prepared to get back to base camp the same day, rather than resting at Camp 2. This is because there is a risk that the jet stream[2] might hit Manaslu. If it does then we don't want to be stranded at Camp 2. This, I think to myself, is Phil doing his old trick of pushing everyone exceptionally hard and assuming we're as strong as he is. There's a hint of *déjà vu*. On Gasherbrum I two years ago, this trick led to Gombu getting his stove out on the way up to Camp 2 because I was too exhausted to go a step further without food and water.

It will be too much for me to go to the summit and back

---

2. A powerful air current that circles the Earth about 10km above its surface.

to base camp in a single day. I don't want to be passing through all the seracs between Camp 1 and Camp 2 in a state of complete exhaustion. Nothing I have done before on a mountain indicates that I will be remotely capable of performing such a feat. I don't want to be bullied into it like I was that day in Pakistan. I made this point in no uncertain terms during our meeting yesterday, and I can't help thinking about it as I lie awake.

Then another thought occurs. Why on earth are we even thinking about setting out for the summit on the day the jet stream is forecast to strike? If it's forecast to arrive on the 5th then I want to get the hell off the mountain, not set out for the top. To hope to reach it then race the jet stream all the way back to base camp would be reckless in the extreme. It's verging on suicidal. I'm reminded of Arnold Schwarzenegger outrunning a nuclear explosion at the end of the film *Predator*.

I decide to speak to Phil this morning with a clear resolution. My preferred option would be to try and reach the summit on October 4th with most of the Himex climbers. If this isn't possible then I'll go to Camp 4 with the rest of our team, but I will come back down without attempting the summit if the jet stream winds are imminent.

But then a strange thing happens, as though Phil has been reading my thoughts. Before I get anywhere near him, he approaches me to address the same issue.

'Hey, Horrell, I got another forecast this morning, and the good news is the jet stream's going to be even later than we thought, on the 8th or 9th.'

Relief washes over me like a magic balm. At a stroke the worries that kept me awake have evaporated. Not only that, but it looks like we've got a proper summit window now, rather than a marginal one.

It's a little more overcast today, but the sky clears as the morning passes. After breakfast I go for a walk up to Crampton Point with Mark and Ian. This is the start of the glacier on the way up to Camp 1, where we've previously had to stop to put on crampons. We originally called it Crampon Point, but Robert decided to name it after Phil, and the name has stuck.

Climbers on the way to Crampton Point

Very little snow has melted, despite the sun, and without crampons the terrain is compact and slippery. A battalion of French climbers is struggling up the rock band. They have big packs on and their progress is slow. Either they are on their summit push before the snow has consolidated, or they're still establishing camps and acclimatising. Either way they seem to be the wrong side of a narrow summit window.

We stop and examine the slopes beneath Camp 3 for

avalanches. It's difficult to make out signs of debris, and we don't know whether anything has slid off the route. The French climbers are taking so long to get up the rock band that we decide to turn around and head back to base camp.

Happy hour is a luxury of our base camp routine that I thoroughly enjoy. At four o'clock each day we sit down for cheese, red wine and Pringles. At the appropriate hour today, I peer into the dining tent and half a dozen team members are crowded around Robert's iPad watching *Groundhog Day*. I return at 4.30 and they're still at it. Phil has told Sarki to cancel happy hour because of them, so I steal a jug of milk tea and biscuits from the dining tent and recline in the comms tent with Mark, Robin and my book. But it's not the same.

This confirms my hatred of TV sets on expeditions, and brings back memories of last year on Cho Oyu. I sat at one end of a crowded dining tent, eating my dinner with a projector in front of me and a big screen swinging against my shoulder – there wasn't enough room for the whole team and a DVD system. After dinner I always had to leave the table and return to my tent so that the rest of my team could watch violent action movies. The one redeeming feature of today is that at least they were watching *Groundhog Day*, which is head and shoulders above any of the crap they watched on Cho Oyu.

At dinner Phil compounds the misery by pretending we've finished the wine. Luckily he doesn't let Sarki in on the joke, and I'm relieved when our trusty cook turns up with a trayful of red.

DAY 28
ANTICIPATION

Friday, 30 September 2011 – Manaslu Base Camp, Nepal

Our last full rest day before the summit push begins in earnest. Some teams are going up today; others have already gone. After breakfast we watch two small figures through binoculars, making their way up the giant snow slope from Camp 2 to Camp 3 below the col. This is the most dangerous part of the climb in terms of avalanche risk. But nothing slides as we watch, and it looks like the snow is consolidating.

Mark, Ian and I take some final pre-summit exercise by wandering a short distance down the moraine ridge towards Samagaon. It's misty again, and we stop just above the vegetation zone. A clear mountain stream of glacial meltwater comes across from the left before spilling down grassy slopes to our right. I feel some nervousness in the pit of my stomach, but mostly I am excited, and full of anticipation now the ascent is upon us. The three of us have climbed a few peaks together and have had our share of bad luck and disappointment upon the 8,000ers. Although we take nothing for granted, this time it feels different – like our chance has finally come. A lot can happen in the next six days, and the weather is always lurking there, ready to ambush us. But I hope this time next week all three of us will have something to celebrate.

We stop and talk for ten minutes before I lead the plod back up to base camp at a pace that is tiring for no one. We need to take it as easy as possible for the next five days leading up to summit day on October 5th.

At dinner, we discuss ways of reducing the weight we'll be carrying up the mountain.

'You may want to think about doing what Anne-Mari and Mila are doing and share a sleeping bag,' Phil says.

The guys around the table look at each other as if Phil is out of his mind. Most of us are frowning.

'What on earth are you talking about?' Steve says.

'Yes, sharing a sleeping bag with Anne-Mari I might be prepared to do,' Mark says, 'but since my tent mate is Mark, the idea is somewhat less appealing.'

Not the least offended, I offer my own thoughts.

'Funnily enough we haven't discussed it, but I think it's safe to say Mark and I won't be sharing a sleeping bag.'

Joking aside, I could be sharing a tent with Marilyn Monroe and I don't think I would scrimp on a sleeping bag. With luck, we will only be climbing for four or five hours a day for the first four days of the summit push. This means we'll be spending a lot of time in our tents resting. Comfort in camp is very important – keeping warm and relaxed with sleeping bag and sleeping mat will make a big difference. Carrying the extra weight for those few short hours of climbing is a price worth paying.

DAY 29
SHORT ROPES

Saturday, 1 October 2011 – Camp 1, Manaslu, Nepal

Mark, Ian and I leave for our summit push straight after lunch, at 12.30. Sarki makes spam and chips with freshly baked bread, cabbage and carrot for lunch. It's tempting to stuff as much down as possible, especially the chips – they're delicious, with spicy seasoned salt. It will help us to build up reserves for the six high-altitude days ahead. But we have nearly 1,000m of climbing to do after lunch, so a light one is definitely what's required.

We pace up the moraine ridge. The others seem content to let me lead as I amble along, conserving energy. The first 300m to Crampton Point was all on rock the first few times we passed this way. But since the storm, snow has covered the trail, and several days of sunshine has done little to melt it.

We continue at our own pace up the glacier until we reach Dislocation Crack. Here we encounter a bottleneck. An elderly Japanese woman is being short-roped up to Camp 1. This is a controversial technique that involves a Sherpa dragging his client by a short length of rope. It's valid on the way down as a means of helping an exhausted climber back to base camp, but some people consider it unnecessary and dangerous on the way up, as it's exhausting for both client and Sherpa. We're only 500m above base camp and there are nearly 3,000m of climbing to the summit. It's clear she has made no attempt to climb the mountain under her own steam, and has adopted a deliberate policy of being short-roped all the way up.

We overtake, but pass two more short-roped climbers further on. They carry banners announcing that they've been sponsored to raise money for victims of the Japanese earthquake earlier this year. It's a worthy cause. Manaslu is a Japanese mountain – it was first explored and climbed by Japanese teams in the 1950s. But I wonder whether they should have chosen an easier mountain for their fundraising, or been in better shape for this one.

Having said that, we're all receiving assistance from Sherpas. The rest of us may be climbing under our own steam, but we're happily clipping in to ropes the Sherpas have fixed and allowing them to carry our tents and oxygen bottles. While most climbers would be embarrassed by the idea of being short-roped, it seems more acceptable to Japanese and Chinese climbers; they have no issues with it.

Shortly before we reach Russell's lower Camp 1, I look back and see that despite my slow pace, Mark has dropped behind. I don't think he wants us to wait for him, though, and we continue onwards as the sun drops behind Manaslu's North Peak. It's a cold evening. As the East Pinnacle rises sharply above the rocks beneath Camp 1, it occurs to me that I'm still waiting for a good view of the main summit.

We reach Camp 1 at four o'clock. It's a strange sight. Snow must have buried many of the tents here, and they've been dug out in such a way that they're now reclining in pits sunk two metres deep.

Mark arrives half an hour behind us. He complains of running out of energy, and as he rests and recovers I boil up plenty of water for both of us. I remind him that it doesn't matter how long it takes, as long as he feels well enough to keep plodding.

Camp is bustling today, much busier than previous times we've been here, and I drift off at seven o'clock to the buzz of voices all around.

DAY 30
PUFFING AND PANTING

Sunday, 2 October 2011 – Camp 2, Manaslu, Nepal

At six o'clock in the morning it's 0°C inside our tent at 5,770m. This isn't as cold as I'm expecting it to be. At 6.15 I lean forward and light the stove. This sometimes takes a particular technique at high altitude where oxygen is scarce. I seem to have taken on the job of lighting while Mark does most of the snow melting once the stove is rumbling.

We have no need to hurry this morning, since our Sherpas are in base camp and need to get to Camp 2 ahead of us to pitch camp. It comes as no surprise when we hear their voices outside our tents at 7.15. They left base camp at five o'clock and are passing through Camp 1 well ahead of us.

I leave with Mark and Mila at eight o'clock. The sky is a little overcast, which makes it easier for us. Although many people left Camp 1 in the small hours this morning, it isn't long before we catch some of them up. Most of the slower climbers are Chinese or Japanese, and some of them don't have a high regard for mountain safety. At the beginning of the ascent to Camp 2, there is a long, flat traverse beneath some seracs. Because of the random nature of serac collapse, this is probably the most dangerous part of the climb to Camp 2. It's an area you want to move through quickly, but I pass a Japanese man who has stopped to film me with his video camera. He hasn't clipped in to the fixed rope, and isn't paying attention to his feet as he films me. He stands in my way, and I have to point out to him that his crampons are snagged in the rope. A little beyond, two more climbers have stopped to rest underneath the seracs.

We continue onwards. The most sustained section of climbing follows, nearly 200m up the Hourglass. It lives up to its name this morning, and there is quite a bottleneck of climbers. I catch up with Robin and Ian, and they look round awkwardly. Someone above them is making the sort of noises you might expect to hear in a bedroom.

We reach the top of the Hourglass at 9.15 and rest for a few minutes on a small platform before the next section of seracs. I walk the rest of today's ascent with Mila and Steve; again they seem content to let me set the pace. The ladder section is easy this time because someone has stretched a couple of taut ropes either side to act as handrails. I'm able to walk across without resorting to the indignity of getting down on all fours.

There is another taut rope a little above that isn't so helpful – it goes right up the middle of an ice chimney. About halfway up I realise I'm going to have to cross over it somehow, but it's much too far away from the ice for me to swing my leg over. I detach my jumar and crawl underneath. Mila, who is climbing behind me, has to lift the rope to get it over my rucksack. Now my safety carabiner is on the wrong side, but there's not enough room in the ice chimney for me to twist around and move it. The rope is too tight to reattach my jumar, so I have to unclip my carabiner from the rope and climb a few steps, secured by just my feet and ice axe, until I'm able to reattach. I struggle exhausted to the top, then wait on a snow balcony above while Mila, Steve and Robin catch up with me. Each one of them emerges exhausted too.

Ascending the Hourglass during the summit push

Most of the harder climbing ends not far above this. Afterwards, it's a slow plod into camp, but towards the top of the climb, in a moment of self-consciousness, I realise that I'm making embarrassing noises, too. I blush and look behind me. Mila and Steve are right on my heels, but they say nothing.

We arrive at 11.30. My lungs are throbbing with every breath, but we have taken only three and a half hours – an hour and a half quicker than the previous time.

Mark arrives an hour later, frustrated again.

'I don't get it. The rest of you are all climbing faster now we've rested at base camp, but I now seem to be the slowest person on the mountain.'

'You didn't notice all those people on short ropes you were overtaking?' I say by way of encouragement.

He's far from being the slowest. We may be a little quicker, but he's in good shape. We're not racing each other up this mountain.

One person who is racing is Anne-Mari, the Flying Finn. She arrives at Camp 2 at 1.30, having left base camp at 5.30am and climbed all the way past Camp 1 to get here. We're not surprised to see her here so quickly, but we are surprised when the more leisurely Robert arrives just half an hour later, having also started from base camp.

We spend the afternoon getting our breath back and watching climbers on the big snow slope up to Camp 3. Many of them seem to be skipping Camp 2, but we're quite happy with our easy progress. We relax, rehydrate and force down some dehydrated expedition meals. Mark may be climbing more slowly, but he doesn't seem to be having any trouble eating.

By five o'clock we're dozing off, relaxed and ready for a long rest. Then at 5.30 Phil turns up and all hell breaks loose.

For the next hour he wanders up and down from tent to tent barking orders at everyone. The jet stream's now due on the 6th, he says, so we'll probably have to descend to base camp on summit day (exactly the scenario I had a sleepless night about a few days ago); the tents aren't secure enough, so all the Sherpas are summoned out of their tents to fix more guy ropes; high winds are on the way, so we have to put our boots, packs and stoves inside the tent rather than in the vestibule. Most annoying of all is that after agreeing with the Sherpas to leave at eight o'clock tomorrow, we're now told we have to leave at seven. This means less opportunity to rehydrate and more opportunity to get cold fingers putting on boots, crampons and harness before we set off.

From being completely relaxed, everyone in camp is now on edge. Eventually I put my ear plugs in so that I don't have to listen to him.

DAY 31
TEA WITH A SUPERSTAR

Monday, 3 October 2011 – Camp 3, Manaslu, Nepal

After a restless night of intermittent sleep, I lean forward at 5.30am to light the stove as ice crystals rain down on me from the ceiling of the tent. It's -2°C, which compares favourably with the 0°C at six o'clock yesterday, 600m lower at Camp 1. It takes nearly an hour and a half to get ready, and we start packing our kit as we wait for the water to boil.

During our days at base camp, we've been debating down clothing versus Gore-Tex for the higher part of the climb. In direct sun, climbing in down suits can be much too hot. On the other hand, if we don't wear them then we have to carry them, and they're bulky. Everyone opts for down clothing today. Mark puts on his purple Rab down suit, which Phil thinks makes him look like Barney the dinosaur. I put on my yellow Rab jacket and black Rab salopettes. When I emerge from the tent, I discover Ian is wearing exactly the same, including matching red Scarpa boots. We look like Tweedledum and Tweedledee.

Again our Sherpas must take down the tents at Camp 2, carry them to Camp 3 and re-erect them. Despite this extra work, they will still be quicker than we are. It's a short climb on a broad snow slope from Camp 2 at 6,400m to Camp 3 at 6,750m. I start ambling slowly at 7.15.

Mila has decided I'm an expert pace-setter (for reasons known only to herself) and she seems to have convinced her tent mate Anne-Mari, the Flying Finn, of it too. They both plod slowly behind me. Although I'm able to adopt a regular pace on easy terrain, the best I can manage at this altitude – without killing myself – is nothing more than an exhausted trudge. I spend the morning holding up two people who are much quicker than I am. Every time I stop for a breather, I plead with them to keep going, but each time they rest and wait for me. I feel like a drunkard getting escorted home from the pub.

When we started out, we could see Camp 3 nestling under the col above us, but before long we are climbing in a whiteout. I can barely see ten steps ahead. I plod along, following the footsteps in front of me, and am surprised to stumble into camp at only 9.30.

Two of our Sherpas, Tarke and Pasang Ongchu, are already pitching the tents. By 10.30 everyone has arrived safely and is settling in – everyone, that is, except José and Steve, who have decided to descend. José was feeling ill when he arrived in camp yesterday, but I'm surprised about Steve, who seemed to be strong when he climbed to Camp 2 with us. His decision is a mystery.

Phil is also concerned about Mark, who arrives wearing down mitts and complaining of frozen fingers. Something has been troubling Mark on all three days of the summit push, but this affliction is more serious. He says it's the same problem he had on Aconcagua. If his fingers don't warm up then it means he won't be able to climb without the risk of losing fingers to frostbite. It's not a risk he's prepared to take.

We have almost the whole day to rest and recuperate. We share our tent with Chongba, who spends the afternoon boiling water for us while we lie back and relax. We know that tomorrow is going to be a hard day, twice as long as today's little leg stretch. Chongba doesn't speak much English, but we manage to extract the names of some of the mountains he's climbed: Everest twelve times, Dhaulagiri, Cho Oyu, Kangchenjunga, Baruntse, Pumori, and Annapurna IV. The first four are all 8,000m peaks. He's a superstar climber for sure, but he's never climbed Manaslu. This means that as my summit-day Sherpa, he will be keen for me to reach the top.

We are in awe of his achievements. Mark summarises the situation neatly when Chongba leaves the tent to collect more snow for drinking water.

'He's climbed Everest twelve times, and he's making fucking tea for us.'

Such is the remarkable humility of many Sherpas. They are the elite of high-altitude mountaineering. It's a bit like Usain Bolt popping round to mow your lawn.

DAY 32
THE ENDLESS SNOW SLOPE

Tuesday, 4 October 2011 – Camp 4, Manaslu, Nepal

Today dawns crisp. It's another morning to get cold fingers putting on crampons, but the sky is clear and there's hardly a breath of wind. It would be a beautiful summit day, and many climbers must be making their way up there now. We can only hope the weather is similar tomorrow. In the meantime, we still have a long day ahead of us at an extreme altitude. We are starting from 6,750m, and hope to climb to something over 7,400m.

We set off at 7.30 on a path which leads horizontally beneath a serac that protects our camp. It curls steeply upwards, around and over, until it reaches Manaslu's broad North Col not far above Camp 3. A small number of mainly Japanese climbers have pitched a slightly higher camp away from the serac. This camp is more exposed to the wind, but I did wonder about that serac. It protected us from gales, but what if it collapsed? We would have been crushed underneath. I'm not experienced enough at this game to know which seracs are considered safe and which are not. I trust Phil to make the right decision.

Although the going is straightforward at this point, the

extreme altitude is taking its toll. We plod slowly with frequent rest stops. Many teams left camp at around the same time; a long conga line of people crawls up to the col and beyond. In our team, Anne-Mari and Mila left first and are somewhere up towards the front of this line. The rest of us take it more leisurely, and keep passing one another as we stop for regular rests and drink breaks.

I hear Phil bark an order at Mark as he approaches us. The latter has taken his gloves off in order to get the wrapper off a snack. This is exactly what he shouldn't be doing with his frozen fingers. We rapidly converge on him, telling him to ask us for help if he needs to do anything that requires manual dexterity.

At the col the path turns left to climb a huge 45° snow slope. It slants left again at the top and passes between some seracs before resuming its inexorable ascent to Camp 4. There is nothing technically difficult about this route, but it continues its slow rise for hours, with no discernible change of scenery. Often in the early stages I keep thinking I've made progress, only to look back and see that I still appear to be near the bottom of this massive slope. I end up calling it the 'endless snow slope'.

I get a better measure of progress by looking beyond the col to Manaslu's North Peak rising the other side. This impressive narrow ridge of a mountain rises to 7,157m, around 250m above the level of the col. Its western side appears just about climbable on horribly steep snow slopes. But these slopes look much too sheer to arrest on in the event of a slide. The crest of the ridge is dangerously corniced all the way along. On its eastern side it gives way dramatically to sheer fluted ice walls. Its summit is a long way above the col and it would be a hard and rewarding slog to get to its peak. By the time we reach the seracs at the top of the endless snow slope, we'll be some distance above it.

On the North Col with the North Peak, also known as
Manaslu North (7,157m), behind

We make progress little by little, but then there's a disheartening setback. Ian and Mark are resting on the slopes above me, and Ian is on the radio to Phil a few dozen metres higher up the hill. It's not getting any warmer here at 7,000m, and it will be colder still at Camp 4 hundreds of metres above. Mark has decided that it's time for him to descend.

'I'm not sacrificing a finger for this mountain,' he says.

I'm gutted for him. Between us, Mark, Ian and I have made eight attempts to climb 8,000m peaks, some of them together. We've had some terrible luck with the weather, but this year seemed to be the one. We were all together at the right time, fit and strong. There was a weather window, and surely we would seize the opportunity and reach the top. Mark's summit push has been fraught with minor difficulties, but even so, I felt sure he was going to hold it all together and keep going.

It's hard to describe how disappointed I am. I still feel confident we'll get there, but it won't be the same without Mark. Phil decides to descend with him. He's climbed Manaslu before, and he wants his Sherpas to reach the summit, rather than face the disappointment of descending with a client. He comes down the slope to join us, but for me the show goes on. I say my goodbyes to Mark and Phil and continue my weary plod.

We seem to be falling one by one. Some way above this, I see Robert sit down and take his ski boots off. He removes his socks, and by the time I reach him, his naked foot is nestling inside Gombu's down jacket. Gombu is trying to get some feeling back into Robert's toes by warming them against his chest. Once again I find myself saluting Sherpas for their self-sacrifice. None of us have envied Robert's decision to ski down Manaslu. His skis are heavy and he's usually been behind us, carrying them on his back. There are many technical sections on the mountain that only the best skiers can pass, and it looks no fun at all. But Robert's biggest worry has been his feet – his technical ski boots are not as warm as our solid mountaineering boots, which are designed for extreme cold. Mark has quit because of frozen fingers – is Robert about to quit with frozen toes?

One person still feeling heated is Robin, but in a different sense. Ahead of us another climber stops for a rest. Rather than unclipping from the rope and moving off the path to make a seat for himself in a bed of thick snow, he remains clipped in to the rope in the middle of the path. Everyone has to unclip and climb around him. Robin is not impressed and lets him know.

'You could jolly well get off the path and let us all past,' he says.

Jolly well? Robin has lived in Canada for many years, but he's not yet cured himself of his essential Englishness. The climber ignores him.

Just as we're reaching the seracs, one of the short-roped Japanese climbers gets stuck. I use the word 'climbers' loosely and in its most generous sense. This particular climber appears to be unable to climb. Instead of an ice axe, she carries two walking poles, and she is struggling to mount one of the footsteps in the snow. She lies flat on her stomach against the 45° slope, squirming like a spider trying to get out of a bathtub. I know she has shorter legs than I do, but all she needs to do is stand up straight and take a big step, like she's climbing the stairs.

She has come to a standstill. Queues of people are stacking up behind her. Once again it's Robin who bellows up the hill for her to move out of the way. We're at a steeper section now, and because she's being short-roped – attached to her Sherpa by a 2m cord – she's not clipped in to the main fixed rope like everyone else. Her Sherpa has to unclip to let everyone by. We pass him one by one, and he looks worried – if she falls, then he's somehow got to hold them both.

Just beneath the seracs we have a slightly more tiring section to climb. Then we find ourselves on a snow ledge leading off to the left. We have reached the top of the endless snow slope, but there's no respite. Within a few metres, the trail curls upwards every bit as steeply. We pass through the seracs, and come to another short snow slope, then more seracs. Then, just when we think we're reaching camp, there's another deceptively long and frustrating hill. The horizon is only ten metres above me. For a desperately long time it remains there, and I never seem to get any closer to it. Is it ever going to end?

But eventually the slope levels out a little. I pass my friend Pierre coming the other way – he's just been to the summit without oxygen, a great achievement. It's hard to know which of us is more exhausted. We have a weary conversation; we're both elated, but I wish we didn't have to talk right now. I imagine he feels the same.

'If you make it, let's both celebrate at base camp,' he says.

'Or better still, we'll have a beer in Kathmandu,' I reply.

After he's gone I remember that Pierre doesn't drink, but I don't suppose it matters.

A few metres before I reach Camp 4 I get my first view of Manaslu's main summit. I've been more than a month on the mountain, and I can't believe this is the first time I've seen it. Even then, I would have missed it, but Gombu is walking behind me and he points it out. Off to the left is the East Pinnacle, which has been hiding the main summit all these weeks. Beyond the pinnacle a three-pronged fortress of rock rises up, and the last of the prongs is the long-cherished summit of Manaslu. Between us and the fortress the route seems to be little more than a long snow plateau. It doesn't look very far at all now.

It's 2.30 and we've been climbing for seven hours. I was expecting a tough day and this was tougher, but she's only a stone's throw away. The weather couldn't be better. Tomorrow, surely!

I'm one of the last of our group into Camp 4, which stands at 7,460m on a balcony of snow. Behind the balcony is the summit plateau, and in front a blanket of cloud floats over the Himalayas. Somewhere beneath those clouds is the rest of the world, stretching for ever. It's a fabulous setting.

'I'm glad I don't have to climb all that again,' I say as I arrive.

Robert has made it too, though we're both sick with exhaustion. I kneel beside the tent and retch, but nothing much comes out. With Mark absent, I find myself sharing a tent with Chongba and Tarke. The latter is my old companion from Gasherbrum, and he greets me with a warm smile. As I stagger into the vestibule, Chongba tries to remove my boots, but I stop him.

'You've climbed Everest twelve times, Chongba. You don't have to take my boots off.'

But I expect that within twenty-four hours, this bold statement will be forgotten, and I will be thanking Chongba for every little gesture that he makes.

He cooks me chicken soup and boils up some water. Then, at four o'clock, I settle into my sleeping bag to grab what sleep I can before our midnight start.

DAY 33
OXYGEN

Wednesday, 5 October 2011, part 1 – Summit day, Manaslu,
Nepal

Just before midnight, I hear Sherpa voices all around me,
talking to one another from tent to tent. Tarke sits up,
barks something through the wall, then lies back down
again. The wind seems to have increased and our tents are
flapping violently. He tells me it's too windy to leave now
as it will be very cold. It will be better for us to leave at
3am. I go back to sleep and snooze a little longer. At 3am
the same thing happens again. The Sherpas talk through
the walls, but it doesn't seem to be any less windy. This
time I don't even bother to ask Tarke the outcome of their
discussion. If it's time to leave then he will wake me.

He does so at 5.45 – without warning. It's beginning to
get light, and the wind seems to be buffeting just as much
as it ever did. I wonder briefly if I will be thwarted by the
weather again, or if we will stay an extra day here at Camp
4, but in the end it's not an issue.

'Are you ready? We are going,' Tarke says.

'Where?'

'Up.' He points at the ceiling.

I spring into action. I'm not ready, of course, but I don't have much to do before I am. I'm wearing most of my clothes inside my sleeping bag, including clean socks, inner boots, trousers, down salopettes, base layer and fleece. The only things I have to put on are down jacket and gloves.

I have very little to carry in my rucksack, and I prepared it yesterday before I went to sleep: just spare gloves, snow goggles and medical kit. And of course, my oxygen bottle, but Chongba is going to sort that outside the tent. All I have left to do is fish out the things I was keeping warm inside my sleeping bag to stop them freezing, and put them in the pockets of my down jacket. There are many of these: water bottles, sun cream, radio, camera and spare batteries, head torch and spare head torch. These last two aren't going to be needed now it's nearly light, but I pack them anyway. You never know. I put on my harness inside the tent, then struggle into my boots in the porch.

It doesn't seem to be as windy once I'm outside. In fact, it's crisp and clear – a beautiful summit morning. Chongba is waiting with the oxygen bottle. He puts it in my pack and fits the mask to my face, setting the flow rate to two litres per minute. This will provide enough for eight hours. Depending on our speed, this should get us to the summit and a little way back again.

Then, without my asking, he bends down to put my crampons on for me. I wasn't expecting this, but I'm grateful. He doesn't seem to feel the cold as much as I do. It's bitterly cold out here, and the manual dexterity needed to put on crampons would mean starting out with freezing fingers. Even with Chongba's help my fingers and toes feel like icicles when we leave at 6.05.

Anne-Mari is still getting ready. As I pass her, I see several climbers from another team leaving ahead of me. A small rise takes us out of the campsite before the start of a long, flat plateau. Beyond this, I can see several steeper banks of snow to climb before we reach the summit fortress.

The oxygen mask feels constricting on my face as I plod slowly onwards. I don't feel like I'm getting any benefit from it. I can't feel any gas coming in, and sometimes it makes a vacuum across my nose and mouth.

What on earth is happening? Nobody told me I would be smothered by a rubber mask a few steps out of high camp.

I panic, and have to move the mask to avoid suffocating. A breath of ambient air squeezes under the rubber and I relax as I'm able to breathe again. This isn't the way it's meant to be. I'm supposed to feel better breathing oxygen from the bottle, not breathing the air from outside.

I continue a few steps at a time, then pause to take a breath. It's the same pace I've been adopting without oxygen, and it will make for a long summit day – how long I don't know – but I intend to continue regardless. By now the people who left camp before me have disappeared across the plateau, and a couple more overtake. Ian appears behind me without his Sherpa, Kami, who was sick as they were leaving camp and told Ian to start without him. As I stop to let him pass, Chongba decides to check my oxygen. He fiddles about behind my neck. I assume he is fixing a blockage in the tube, but later it occurs to me that he may have turned up the flow rate.

Whatever he did, I suddenly feel great. I start going like the clappers. I walk faster, and continue without stopping.

We leave Ian behind and overtake the people who previously passed us.

I reach the back of the plateau and begin ascending the first of the steep banks of snow, a hundred metres or more in height. I race up it, Chongba behind me. There's still a long way to go, but now I feel sure we'll reach the summit.

And it's not only that I seem to feel more energy. Gradually my fingers and toes begin to warm up. They become very painful as I start to get feeling back into them, but digit by digit the pain vanishes, and it's not long before they feel comfortable again. It's the magic effect of oxygen reaching my extremities. One of the more important benefits of bottled oxygen many people don't realise is that it helps to combat frostbite on a cold summit day.

I've gained confidence now and I start to pay attention to some of the conversations firing off from the radio in my pocket. I learn that Mila is worried about her cold fingers and has decided not to ascend. This is both surprising and disappointing, as she's been strong all along. Less of a shock is that Robert is also having doubts about the cold.

We reach the top of the first snow bank and find ourselves on another long snow plateau. This one slopes upwards more steeply, and is more tiring to cross. I stop halfway up it for water. I'm not sure how to drink with my oxygen mask on, but Chongba helps, taking the mask off my face and putting it back on again when I've finished drinking.

When we start moving again, my climbing is much more laboured. It's as if the magic effects of the oxygen have vanished. I don't have the difficulties that I experienced at the start, but I no longer fly like the wind. From now on, it's hard graft – exactly what I expected an 8,000m summit day to be like.

At the end of the second plateau there's another hundred-metre snow bank, slanting up steeply. Its surface is hard and crusty, and I make my way up it in small steps. A line of fixed rope lies on the ground beneath my feet, but my brain is not working to full capacity. It would be an easy thing to clip my carabiner into the rope for safety, but I believe I'm making good progress, and decide I don't need to.

Only when I reach the top do I realise that I'm faltering. I sit down for another rest. Ian overtakes for a second time, still climbing on his own, without Kami.

I look up at a third snow plateau ahead of us. It slants nearly as steeply as the two snow banks that preceded it, but at the top end of it is the summit fortress. We're getting very close now. I just need to make it up this slope, and I will be standing at the base of Manaslu's rocky crown.

I plod slowly, pausing frequently. The snow is powdery, and the footsteps of those who came before me are often deep. Ian charges ahead and waits for us at the end of the plateau, where a flattish area of snow forms a good resting place before the final summit haul. Chongba decides it's a good moment to change my oxygen bottle. Ian asks him about Kami, who is carrying his second cylinder. On the radio, Chongba learns that Kami is coming, but he's still some way away, so he checks Ian's oxygen himself and confirms that there's still enough to reach the summit.

We press on up the final summit rampart. Ian moves ahead again. He's much quicker than me, but now we're so close I'm content to continue at whatever pace I can muster. This section is much steeper, and I remember to clip in to the fixed rope. I'm sure I would be able to arrest myself with my axe here, but to fall now would be silly – not just because it would scare the crap out of me. I would have to climb back up again, expending unnecessary energy.

Climbers are coming back down from the summit. This makes things difficult because one of us has to unclip and move out of the way. Both parties are exhausted and there's no protocol; sometimes I move, and other times I wait for the other person to stand aside. Sometimes neither of us moves and a stand-off ensues.

Nobody says a word. I should be congratulating them on their summit success, but I still have my own battle ahead of me and I remain silent. I recognise no one, but it's difficult when people are wearing snow goggles and oxygen masks. I can't be bothered to concentrate too hard on identifying anyone.

There's a short snow couloir just beneath the summit crown. I see Ian waiting at the top, beckoning frantically. This irritates me. It's perfectly clear that I'm coming up, but there's no way I'm going to go any quicker. I ignore him and concentrate on my feet.

A surprise awaits me at the top of the couloir. Ian is holding his oxygen mask to the face of a bearded man in a red down suit. So that's why he was gesturing for me to come quickly. Another climber is in trouble, but what does he expect me to do? I flop down in the snow beside them and get my breath back.

Chongba arrives and taps me on the shoulder.

'Look, the summit!' he says.

I look up, and see that I'm sitting in an area no more than a hundred metres in length. The trail passes to the left through a bed of snow, and to the right three triangular summits rise up in a line. The first two are minor snow domes, no more than a few metres high, but the one at the back is a little more complex. At the far end of this narrow platform of snow, its snake-like summit ridge forms a spine of snow zigzagging up to a crown of rock. From this short distance I can see that the rock is decked in prayer flags.

It's the true summit of Manaslu, barely a stone's throw away. At sea level I could run up it in sixty seconds. But at this altitude, exhausted as I am, it will probably take another ten to fifteen minutes to reach it. Having waited patiently for many weeks, and battled hard for five days to get here, it's my only focus right now. I don't need any distractions like rescues to carry out – at least not until after I've reached it.

After a short breather, I stand up and continue. Chongba somehow persuades Ian to leave the bearded man for now, and continue with us. At the foot of the ridge I take a few seconds to prepare my camera for a summit photo. I put it in an accessible pocket of my down jacket and warm up the batteries.

Two people have preceded us up the ridge, but Chongba decides they won't get in our way. We continue slowly behind them, and arrive on the summit just as they are leaving.[3]

Once they are gone we have the summit to ourselves. Ian waits a little below, at a place where they can pass. He is there for a long time, and only moves up to join us after we've taken our summit photos. I look back and ask Chongba why he's still waiting. Ian seems more exhausted and subdued now, perhaps because his mask was off for some time at the top of the couloir as he gave his precious

---

3. These two climbers were Karel and Chedar, another of our Sherpas. I discovered this a few days after the expedition when Karel sent me his photos from the trip. There in the background of a shot of Chedar standing on the summit, with a sea of snow-capped peaks behind him, were three golden figures making their way up the ridge below – me, Chongba and Ian.

oxygen to someone else.

It's 11.30 and he doesn't want to stay on the summit. As soon as we've taken his photo he asks us to leave. I'm elated about our success, but I'm not too keen to stick around either – it's tight and exposed up here, and three people is a bit of a crowd.

As we are leaving I hear Phil's voice come over the radio to ask us where we are. I scream back that we're on the summit, but I don't think he hears me.

The day is not over, and we still have a long way to go.

Mark Horrell on the main summit of Manaslu (8,163m),
the eighth-highest mountain in the world

DAY 33
BACKPACK

Wednesday, 5 October 2011, part 2 – Summit day, Manaslu, Nepal

We get down from the exposed section and stop to rest at the top of the snow couloir. As I clean my snow goggles, which iced up when I removed them for the summit photo, Anne-Mari appears from the top of the couloir with Pasang Ongchu and Kami. She's not using oxygen, but she seems to be in better shape than we are. She is alert enough to congratulate us on reaching the top.

The three of them pass by to complete the last few steps to the summit. We begin our long descent, which comes to an abrupt halt a short way down the second fixed rope. There, sitting motionless in the snow, is the bearded man. He has descended little more than fifty metres since Ian left him to come with us to the summit, but at least that's something.

Chongba wants to continue – his responsibility is to get me down safely – but the man looks distraught. I realise we can't leave him here with so few people behind us, but helping him proves a challenge. My first thought is to find out what team he belongs to, and try to establish contact with them on the radio. But he doesn't speak any English, and each time I ask him a question, he barks back at me in what I think is Spanish.

Anne-Mari on the summit crown, with the subsidiary summits on the right and true summit at the far end

I estimate that he's in his fifties or sixties, and judging by the large number of logos stitched to his down suit, I guess that he may be a professional climber. When I produce my radio he asks for Monica, the team doctor with Russell Brice's Himex team. She was the one who put Ian's shoulder back in place when he dislocated it earlier in the expedition. I don't believe this man is climbing with Himex, but perhaps he just wants me to call Monica for advice.

I decide to contact Phil in base camp, but I get no response from the radio.[4] I look at my medical kit and pull

___
4. I learned later that there was a dead zone for reception just below the summit.

out something marked 'AMS' (for Acute Mountain Sickness). It's Diamox, a drug to help with acclimatisation. Although it won't do him any harm, it's not the drug we need to get him moving again.

In any case, he's not interested in the drug. He starts pointing excitedly at my oxygen mask. This is the magic potion that he wants. OK, I think to myself, I was hoping to use my oxygen to descend, but it hasn't killed me when I've taken my mask off to drink or use the radio. Perhaps I can descend without it – and this man needs it more than I do.

I reach for my mask, but Chongba protests. He doesn't want me to give my oxygen up. He offers to take the man's rucksack instead, but again the man isn't interested. I become exasperated. It's as if we're only allowed to rescue him on his own terms.

I had forgotten Ian, who has been quiet these last few minutes. He steps into the conversation and becomes animated again.

'It's OK, Mark, I will do it. He can have my oxygen,' he says.

Knowing Ian as I do, I realise there is no point arguing about which of us is going to make the sacrifice. He will win that argument. It seems there is nothing more I can do to help. I leave Ian to it and continue my descent. A few moments later I feel Chongba's steps behind me.

We reach the bottom of the summit fortress and begin descending the third snow plateau, where we pass two figures still climbing. The first is tired and ignores me, but the second, a Sherpa carrying a pair of skis, stops me and holds his mittened hand out with a big smile on his face. It's Gombu and Robert – they haven't got far to go now. Robert must have decided to wait until it was warmer before starting out. It's a brave decision which means he can ascend more safely in his thinner ski boots. But it also means he will be arriving late on the summit, with a long descent ahead of him.

The rest of the descent to Camp 4 is straightforward, but excruciating. I must have been carrying my pack in an awkward posture all the way up. Now that we're descending, my neck and shoulders are screaming in pain. More awkwardly, I can't seem to keep my oxygen mask in place on my face. If I stand up straight, the tube is too short, and pulls the mask down to my chin. I can only keep the mask attached to my nose and mouth if I stoop, and I realise I must have been walking like this most of the way up. To ease the pain I hold my neck up straight, but this means I have to hold the mask in position with my hand. By the time we reach Camp 4 at two o'clock, I can't wait to get the whole apparatus off.

Chedar is waiting by the tents and congratulates me as I approach.

'You are strong man,' he says.

It's nice of him, but I know it's not true. I certainly don't feel it. I needed two bottles of oxygen and a lot of help from Chongba. Without them, I doubt I would have been strong enough.

Nor do I feel elated any longer, though I did on the summit. We're still at 7,460m and have a long way to descend before we're safe. I have a short rest in the tent then pack away my things for an immediate descent to Camp 2, 1,000m below us.

We're only a short way through a busy day, and it's going to get much worse.

By three o'clock I'm ready to leave with a much larger pack. Our Sherpas want me to use the rest of my oxygen, but with the problems and pain I experienced on the way down I have no intention of doing so. Besides, there's no room in my pack for the 3½kg bottle. They look annoyed. It doesn't occur to me that if I don't carry it, then somebody else will have to.

I leave in a group with Ian and Anne-Mari, who arrived in Camp 4 not long after me. My heavier pack continues to give me discomfort; I'm exhausted, and vaguely aware that the pack is badly adjusted and hanging sideways, but the steep slopes below Camp 4 are no place to stop and try to figure it out. Anne-Mari and Ian are quick and disappear ahead of me. The steps in the snow have turned to powder in the late afternoon sun, and fall away beneath me. I have to concentrate with every step, and I feel certain I'm going to fall.

It happens on the steep traverse between seracs, just before the endless snow slope, and it leaves me in shock.

It has taken me over an hour to get that far. I have to sit down and rest every few steps. For the first time I start to get concerned about the time – I have only 3½ hours of daylight for the whole descent from Camp 4 to Camp 2. I feel like I've only come a fraction of the way, and I'm starting to panic. That long snow slope looks daunting.

I'm arm-wrapping down a fixed rope when I fall. My hand becomes trapped in a taut rope which bears my falling weight. My safety carabiner is also attached to the rope, and somehow I've been able to arrest myself with my axe. These three things between them have held my fall, but it's exhausting to raise myself back into position, and I'm badly shaken. Far below me on the slopes down to the col, some of our Sherpas may have been watching. I see them stop and look at me for a long time – either they saw me fall or watched me haul myself back onto the trail in laboured fashion. It occurs to me that the group could include Ian and Anne-Mari, miles ahead and wondering how the hell I'm now so far behind them.

At the top of the long descent to the col I stop in the first flat place I have reached since leaving Camp 4. I contemplate an alternative solution to get me down before dark. It's a vast slope, and if I toboggan down I'll be going a million miles an hour by the time I reach the bottom. There are people descending below me, and I don't want them to see me or put them in any danger, but perhaps a controlled slide for short sections might be possible.

My pack has become a real problem – I think about attaching it to a carabiner and sliding it down the fixed rope. While I consider this, Pasang Ongchu and a number of other climbers come by. This ends my plan of executing a controlled slide, because they will be in the way, but Pasang Ongchu agrees to help me give the rucksack idea a try. It bounces a short way and keeps stopping in the snow, yet somehow he is able to manoeuvre it down below me.

My own descent of this impossibly long slope is much slower. Before long all the other climbers are way ahead of me and becoming smaller as they disappear into the distance. I do a few controlled slides using my ice axe as a brake in places where it's safer to do so. At other times I can only walk, stopping frequently to rest.

As everyone else vanishes, the faithful and reliable Pasang Ongchu lingers, looking up at me to check that I'm safe. When I reach the higher Camp 3 just below the col, where the Japanese climbers have their tents, he is waiting with my rucksack. I have no idea how he got it here – his own pack is considerably bigger and it's clear he can't carry both of them.

It's six o'clock and dusk is approaching. He asks me to

speak to Phil on the radio, who has had a nervous day at base camp following our progress. Physically exhausted as I am, I'm fully aware of the situation I find myself in. I talk lucidly to Phil about what's required, and this seems to reassure him.

'I'm knackered, but I'll put the head torch on and keep plodding, even if it takes another two hours. We'll just have to keep going till eight o'clock.'

He tells me Pasang Ongchu will stay with me till we reach camp. I pull my head torch out and examine the straps of my pack. Immediately I can see what the problem is: one of the shoulder straps is about 30cm longer than the other. No wonder the pack was hanging sideways. If only I had noticed this when we set out at six o'clock this morning, how much easier everything would have been.

I've finished the last of my water and I ask Pasang Ongchu if he has any left. He hasn't, but he radios to Chongba to bring some up from Camp 2. My pack is now much easier to carry, and although I'm still slow, I can continue with regular rests. Pasang Ongchu bears these with infinite patience.

As it gets colder, the snow becomes crisp and firm again, making things much easier underfoot. We can see Chongba's head torch on the slopes below, inching its way up towards us. It acts like a beacon and spurs me on to Camp 2. When we finally catch up with him all is well. I've drunk just a litre of water all day and eaten no food at all. The cold juice he brings acts like magic potion. He shoulders my pack and we reach Camp 2 at 7.30.

It's been a long, long day. I've reached the summit of my first 8,000m peak, yet I'm acutely aware that all is not over. Ian and Robin are still awake and have been waiting up for me. Robin had the kindness to boil a full litre of hot water for me to drink through the night. They shuffle up, I slump in between them, and I fall asleep almost immediately.

DAY 34
AGONY

Thursday, 6 October 2011 – Manaslu Base Camp, Nepal

I'm keen to find out what happened to the rest of our team on summit day. Robin tells me he set off for the summit, but his progress was sluggish. Sangye kept turning up the flow rate on his oxygen until he was walking at the maximum of four litres per minute. This made him stronger, but it meant his oxygen supply was running out more quickly. After three hours of walking he felt he didn't have enough to get him to the summit and back, and decided to turn around. Karel, on the other hand, reached the summit before us with Chedar. We actually saw them on the summit. Robert reached the top with Gombu after we passed them on our way down. And, of course, Ian, Anne-Mari and I made it too. This means that five clients and five Sherpas got to the top, a fair tally of success for Altitude Junkies.

Ian tells me the rest of the strange saga of the bearded man we found on the summit crown. After I left, Ian was still helping him when Anne-Mari passed by with Kami and Pasang Ongchu. The two Sherpas turned him over and Anne-Mari administered a dexamethasone injection into his buttock through his down suit. She's not a doctor and had never done this before, but it got him moving again. With Ian supplying the rest of his oxygen, they probably saved his life. They helped him a short way down, then met one of his own Sherpas coming up with an oxygen cylinder. At this point the other Sherpa took over. Ian and Anne-Mari left them, and reached Camp 4 not long after me.

We still don't know who he is, but something about his attitude bothered me. He seemed demanding and ungrateful. Is this what high-altitude cerebral edema (HACE) does to you, or is he always like that?

Outside our tent I hear signs of activity. Anne-Mari sticks her head through the door to pick up a helmet she left here on the way up. We hear Karel and Robert getting ready, and all of them are away early. Robin, Ian and I are in no hurry, but we know the Sherpas will want to pack away our tent, so we can't keep them waiting too long. Gombu pokes his head in to offer some boiled water. This saves us the bother of getting a stove working ourselves. We take the hint, rise up and start packing.

By nine o'clock we're ready to leave for the 1,600m descent to base camp – 1,600m that I'm quite nervous about. It's the most technically challenging part of the climb and I've singled out three sections that might cause difficulties for an exhausted climber: the ice chimney with the tight rope stretched through it, the crevasse with the ladder, and the 200m Hourglass. This third and final hazard hopefully won't have too many climbers on it today, but it's precipitous and tiring, and has a crevasse of its own halfway down.

Ian speeds ahead early on, as is his habit, but Robin and I agree to take it slowly. We take frequent rests to minimise the chance of making mistakes in our worn-out state. Many Sherpas from the Himex team are coming up to pack away their higher camps. We stop and wait patiently for them to pass. By the time we reach the awkward sections, our own Sherpas have dismantled Camp 2 and caught up with us, so we descend together. The ice chimney is straightforward without anyone below me keeping the rope taut. It takes concentration, but I descend it without difficulty. The ladder is also no problem. Before long we find ourselves stopping for a rest at the top of the Hourglass.

Approaching Camp 1 during the descent

After five minutes most of the Sherpas move on, but Sangye waits to keep an eye on Robin and me. I leave first. The steps are collapsing again and it's hard work, but I maintain my concentration and jump over the big crevasse as I descend. At the bottom there's no place for me to stop, rest and congratulate myself – I'm in a dangerous place with many seracs above me. I stagger along the traverse beneath them and stumble into Camp 1 at 11.15.

Ian has been waiting for us, and we rest for another fifteen minutes. Tarke, who is helping to pack away Camp 1, brings over some tinned peaches, the first food I've had for nearly forty-eight hours. It's impossible to describe how beautiful they are, and their sugary juice slides down my throat like nectar. I look up at the serac maze above Camp 1. It's another great day, but I'm glad we've made it through this section, and relieved I'll never need to go up it again.

The rest of the descent is more straightforward, but it's still going to be hard for me. At 11.30 we shoulder our packs for the final slog. My neck and shoulders cry in agony, and I can only move for a few hundred yards before having to stop and put my pack down. Ian and Robin are in better shape. They seem to be content to rest frequently as we cross the glacier in a series of staggered leaps.

I fight a mental battle with every step. Each time I get up and continue, I focus my mind on going as far as I can before I need to stop again. Each time I get a little further, and bask in the feeling of knowing I'm that bit closer to base camp.

At the top of the rock band beneath Crampton Point, I need a longer rest. This scramble is the final tricky obstacle and it needs my complete attention. I don't want to do anything silly with the end so close. Robin agrees to wait, but Ian is impatient to get it over with, and goes on ahead. We complete it without mishap and I need another rest at the bottom.

I'm grateful when one of our kitchen boys appears over a brow and offers to take my pack for me. I give it up without protest, but it doesn't seem to matter now. As I creep along the final moraine ridge into base camp, the pain in my neck is almost too much to bear. I change my stance, but there are no comfortable positions for me to hold it in. I massage it as I walk, but this brings only token relief. The best arrangement seems to be staring at my feet in the same stooped posture I must have adopted on summit day. I don't even stagger – I can't stand up straight and I must look a hundred years old to the others watching me as I descend the final ramp of rock into camp.

We arrive at 1.30 and I flop down on a rock step outside the dining tent. No one is cheering. I shake hands with all of them, and they look on blankly as I catch my breath. Perhaps there is a hint of concerned curiosity. I expect they are shocked by my appearance. I feel like a wizened old man, but I'm down in one piece, and that's the only thing that matters.

'How does it feel to conquer an 8,000m peak?' José says.

I don't look up, so I don't know whether he's smirking.

'Conquered, my arse,' I cough. 'Conked out, more like.'

Starving and dehydrated, I head to the dining tent, unsure of what my stomach's going to accept – but chips, spam, and copious quantities of sugary milk tea turn out to be just the ticket. José and I had been intending to head to the Annapurna Sanctuary after the expedition, and perhaps find a trekking peak to climb, but shouldering my pack again for a few days of trekking doesn't seem feasible in my present state. In fact, it sounds preposterous. Poor José, who had some bad luck with illness here, must sense this.

Phil tells us about the bearded man we helped, a famous Spanish climber called Juanito Oiarzabal, who completed all the 8,000ers some time ago and is now trying to be the first person to climb them all twice. Apparently

Russell Brice is no fan of his. He helped Juanito's team out in rather more dramatic fashion on Lhotse only four months ago and received no thanks for it.

I haven't heard of him. He must have been a great climber once; perhaps he still is, and he just had a bad day. But it seems to me that no matter what your achievements, if you need lesser men to save your life then it's wise to behave with humility. It must be embarrassing for a great alpinist to be helped by a group of commercial clients.

Phil's opinion is more neutral, but not entirely. When Juanito's Sherpa comes over to offer money for the oxygen that Ian donated, he refuses payment and is slightly offended.

'It's not the money; it's the principle,' he tells us.

Commercial expedition leaders like Phil and Russell, who do all they can to make the mountain safe for their inexperienced clients, aren't happy when safety is put at risk by climbers on other teams. Had a more serious rescue been necessary then it's likely our Sherpas would have been involved, and we the clients would have been descending on our own – despite paying for the Sherpas to be here.

They also tell me of another moment of comedy that happened during my descent. An anxious Phil was sitting beside the radio in base camp with the rest of the team while Ian kept him updated from the tent at Camp 2.

'I can see Mark's head torch. He's arriving in Camp 2 now.' A pause. 'Er… I don't think that was Mark. He's just walked straight through camp.'

Phil was slapping his amply coiffured forehead in frustration here at base camp. There was nothing he could do to help. Thankfully I arrived in Camp 2 not long after, but I wasn't the last to keep him up. He was unable to go to bed with his mind at ease until Robert, who reached the summit after me, returned to Camp 2 more than an hour later.

My feast of chips and tea in the dining tent is short respite. If I thought I was going to be allowed to rest for a few hours, then I'm in for a shock. At four o'clock Phil tells me the porters will be arriving at breakfast. Tomorrow morning they will take our equipment down to Samagaon for the helicopter flight back to Kathmandu.

Utterly dismayed, I trudge wearily to my tent. I spend the next three hours packing in a daze.

DAY 35
FRIENDSHIP AND ALCOHOL

Friday, 7 October 2011 – Samagaon, Manaslu Circuit, Nepal

The haste continues this morning. It seems that after spending over a month doing everything in our power to get to the top of Manaslu, we can't leave the mountain quickly enough. I want to linger and savour the moment, let it all sink in, but I don't get the opportunity.

I'm bewildered by the hurry. Exhaustion seeps through every bone in my body, and I wish I could lie in my sleeping bag a little while longer now that the ascent is done. But no. The others have already gone by the time I shake hands with Chongba, give him an exhausted bear hug, and thank him for all he's done. I owe my summit success to him more than anyone. Except perhaps Phil. I don't think I would have made it to the summit and back without Chongba. And I certainly wouldn't have made it without all the other support from Sherpas throughout the expedition, fixing the ropes, and carrying tents and equipment to the higher camps.

I pick up my walking stick and head for the moraine ridge down to Samagaon. The next two hours are magical, as blue sky reigns over the Budhi Gandaki valley for the first time since we've been here. At last I can see the ends of the horizon: Samagaon far beneath me; Birendra Tal, the turquoise lake halfway up the hillside; and the strange-looking mountain of Pangbuche towering over everything, in some ways even more dramatic than Manaslu itself.

Behind me the main summit of Manaslu peeps from behind the East Pinnacle. It's the clearest view I've had of it yet. It's a beautiful feeling to have these two hours by myself to appreciate where I am and what I've done. I'm in no hurry to descend.

On the ridge below Manaslu Base Camp,
with Pangbuche rising overhead

When I reach the lodge in Samagaon, the sublime becomes the ridiculous more quickly than the Dalai Lama putting on a pair of comedy breasts. Mark, Ian and Robin are resting in the dining room, and three big, empty bottles of Tuborg beer are already sitting on the table in front of them.

There is nothing I can do but sit down, order a beer of my own, and remain there, ordering more until Mark and Ian allow me to leave. This takes a while. By the end of the day, no fewer than thirty-two empty bottles are decorating the table, and all of us have pledged our undying friendship.

Mark is emotional. Despite his disappointment, he is happy for the rest of us.

'Ian, not only did you get to the summit of an 8,000m peak, but you saved someone's life on the way down. How good is that – you're a hero.'

Ian shifts awkwardly in his chair and shakes his head. 'Let it rest. I'm not a hero.'

'You are. You're a fucking hero.'

I'm not spared the adulation. I look at the photos on my camera and discover that I removed my gloves on the summit.

'You weren't wearing gloves on the summit – that's unbelievable. You're a fucking superman. How do I compete with that, with my frozen fingers? You guys are incredible.'

Ian looks concerned.

'You're not going to give up climbing, are you, just because you didn't get to the summit? I want to keep climbing with you guys.'

When the king of the mountain, Russell Brice, walks into the teahouse on his own, I expect him to take one look at the three drunken Brits, turn around and walk straight out again. Russell, a New Zealander, is the owner of the Himex team who fixed all the ropes on the mountain. He is something of a celebrity in the world of commercial mountaineering. He was one of the first people to guide commercially on Everest, and has pioneered commercial expeditions on many of the 8,000m peaks. The rope fixing and trail breaking of his Himex Sherpas to a certain extent guided the itineraries of every climber on Manaslu this year. This included Altitude Junkies. Phil is a good friend of Russell's, and they discussed tactics on several occasions.

Robin has had the good sense to leave by now, and I'm surprised when Russell spies a spare seat at our table, and decides to join us. He is a controversial figure who often finds himself in the media spotlight. This is sometimes by choice, but not always. I have no idea what sort of person he is, and this is the first time I've seen him at close range. He is grey-haired, and around sixty years old. He seems good-natured and earnest, not the brash Kiwi I was expecting, and I wonder how he acquired his divisive reputation.

He doesn't seem like the sort of person who would relish a barrage of British drunkenness, but in this respect it appears that I'm wrong. He sits down with us at nine o'clock. Perhaps he will stay for one drink, I tell myself, just to humour us. But no, not Russell. He is here for the evening, despite Mark attacking him with questions, like a very drunk chat-show host.

'What's your biggest mistake? Why do you do what you do? Do you still enjoy it?'

Russell answers all these questions with great forbearance. More surprisingly, after a couple of drinks, he manages to find our level. For example, when he learns that Ian is Welsh, he realises that they have a common interest – sheep. He even tells us a couple of sheep jokes, which I intend to add to my library.

He is still there at midnight, when I decide that enough is enough. I'm still exhausted from the climb. I was exhausted when I arrived at the teahouse this morning. The beer hasn't helped, and tomorrow we have to be ready for an early helicopter flight back to Kathmandu. I rise from the table and bid them goodnight.

DAY 36
THE HELICOPTERS

Saturday, 8 October 2011 – Samagaon, Manaslu Circuit, Nepal

There's one last twist in the tale. Little do we know that the most terrifying part of the whole expedition is yet to come.

Just before six o'clock, I'm lying awake on a wooden bed in the teahouse when I hear the rotors of a helicopter buzz overhead. For reasons I've never fully understood, but perhaps related to fuel supplies, helicopter departures in Nepal are always frantic. It's normal to be flying away within a split second of your helicopter landing, having sprinted from a safe location a short distance away and leaped inside. This time I'm confident that this is somebody else's helicopter, and I can lie in bed for a little while longer. Ours is not due to arrive until later in the morning.

But I enjoy the spectacle of watching three inebriated people – Mark, Ian and Robin – wake from a peaceful slumber, and sit bolt upright all in a line. They're still drunk – they're probably still asleep – but within minutes they have dressed, packed and disappeared out of the door before I've even had a chance to tell them that it's not our helicopter. Well, OK, I did have a chance to tell them, but their performance was mesmerising, and I decided to let them go.

I know I can take my time, but I don't want to rise too late. I remember that although I've been here several weeks, I've had few opportunities to see the main summit of Manaslu. Early morning is usually the best time, before the clouds have had time to form as water evaporates from the snow.

I'm not disappointed when I make my way outside. The sky is a deep blue, and there is not a single cloud anywhere. Manaslu rises majestically above a wooded hillside, its twin summits clad in white shawls. The East Pinnacle is the most arresting, as it always has been, a finger of rock protruding above a sheer triangular face of ice. It looks the higher of the two, but I know better now. To its left the broader main summit rises further away from us. Between the two summits I have a clear view of the snow ramp we ascended, slanting at a steady angle right to the very top. I'm so glad I wasn't denied this view. Now I can return home with a complete picture of the mountain.

When our helicopters arrive two hours later, they both try to land on the same tiny helipad, but the second one struggles. Twice it flies over so low that we can see the whites of the pilot's eyes. Each time he tries to lower his aircraft into position, but thinks better of it and aborts the landing.

'The bags, the bags,' the first pilot shouts, who is now on the ground. 'The bags aren't supposed to be here.'

Our duffle bags are piled up on the edge of the landing pad, and getting in the way. We spring into the action, pick up the bags, throw them all down a bank nearby, and jump on top of them. Within seconds the other helicopter has landed in the place where our bags were a moment earlier.

Robert, Karel and Mila jump into the helicopter, and a few random bags are thrown in behind them. We wait patiently for the helicopter to take off again, but something's wrong. It stays where it is.

The pilot signals frantically. The door opens and Mila is pulled out – she's too heavy, the last straw. The pilot tries again, and the helicopter rises a few metres off the ground, hovers, and begins to turn.

It's right above us; if it doesn't have enough lift then we will all be squashed beneath it. I think of those two days of exhausted concentration coming down the mountain, summoning every ounce of my strength, just to survive. Has this all been for nothing? Of all the ways to go, I never imagined I would be flattened like a pizza.

I look up in terror at the helicopter turning just above me, but a moment later I am calm again. There is not much I can do but watch, and hope.

It rotates through 180° and hovers in place for a few seconds, then it disappears down the valley.

I breathe a sigh of relief. The expedition is over, I've reached the summit, and we're all still alive.

The second helicopter leaves in less dramatic fashion. Mark, Ian, Robin and I walk back through the village to the large open area outside the school – a much safer location to land a helicopter. The school is closed today. We lie patiently on the grass as we wait for our transport to make its return flight to Kathmandu.

It's one of those magic moments when it's a joy to be alive.

EPILOGUE

Sunday, 23 September 2012 – Camp 2, Manaslu, Nepal

A year after the events described in this diary, something happened on Manaslu that put our climb into perspective.

At around 4.30am on Sunday, 23 September 2012, a 600m section of ice broke off one of the seracs which cut across the top of the endless snow slope above the North Col. It triggered a huge avalanche which swept down the big snow slope above Camp 2.

It could have happened at any time – night, day, spring, summer, autumn or winter, outside the climbing season, or during it.

It happened during it, on one of those rare occasions when climbers were on the mountain, completing an acclimatisation rotation. Camp 3 was directly in its path. Most of the tents were picked up and hurled down the slope in the direction of Camp 2, with a force that was difficult to comprehend.

The Altitude Junkies team were at Camp 2, in almost the same location we had camped a year earlier. Among them were Mila, on her second attempt, Phil and Dorje.

Their camp was protected from the bulk of the avalanche by the large crevasse alongside it, that funnelled any sliding debris away from camp, but it was blasted by the wind.

Phil was awake in the tent he was sharing with one of his clients. He was fiddling with the zip on his sleeping bag when he heard the avalanche boom above them. A moment later he was struck in the head by the blast. The tent was lifted off the ground and catapulted down the slope, rotating several times. When it came to rest a few metres away, Phil was lying on top of his client, and the tent was destroyed. But they were both alive and unharmed.

Outside, the tents of all the other Junkies clients and Sherpas had suffered the same fate. Mila had also been awake in the tent she was sharing with another client, Edita. They were about to light the stove when Mila heard a rumble.

'An avalanche!' she said with a shudder.

They didn't have much time to ponder before they too were tossed around like a cork. When the tent came to rest, their first thought was that they had been buried alive. It was a great relief when Edita unzipped the door and saw stars above them.

Mercifully, everyone in the team had survived with only minor injuries, such as cuts, bruises and concussion.

It was still dark, and it took them some hours to find enough equipment and clothing to think about descending. On the slopes above them was carnage, with tents among the debris. They knew only too well there would be people too, some who were no longer alive.

While they hunted in the wreckage for their belongings, a Sherpa who had been swept down the mountain from Camp 3 stumbled into their camp with frostbite and head injuries. He had been caught in the slide, and had descended without boots. They looked after him and gave him medication while they waited for a helicopter to come and rescue him.

Meanwhile down at base camp, Russell Brice of Himex had already started coordinating the rescue operation. He called all the radio frequencies that he knew climbers were using on the mountain, to try and establish contact with other teams. He started taking a register of climbers to see who was missing. He called his office in Kathmandu to arrange helicopters. A medical post was set up at the base camp helipad, and his team prepared their own medical tent to be used as a makeshift hospital ward.

During the course of the day, eighteen flights were made between base camp and the rescue site. Russell established that thirty-one people had been caught in the avalanche. The majority of these were either evacuated by helicopter, or were able to evacuate themselves.

But they also recovered eight bodies. Three people were missing, and their bodies were also found over the coming days. Among the eleven casualties were six French, a German, an Italian, a Spanish, a Canadian and a Nepali.

Life went on for those who had survived the avalanche. Some chose to return home; others stayed to continue their expeditions. Nine days after the avalanche, fifteen members of the Altitude Junkies team reached the summit: six clients, eight Sherpas, and Phil. Among them were Mila and Chongba.

How different my expedition might have been had that serac collapsed at another moment. A year earlier, on 23 September 2011, we made our abortive first summit attempt and had to retreat in a snowstorm. It's a reminder that we can never take our lives for granted. I feel blessed to have reached the summit, but it's more of a blessing that

I'm able to climb again.

This book is dedicated to the eleven climbers who died in the 2012 avalanche on Manaslu, and to all those who have lost their lives in the mountains.

But there are many hazards in life and many events beyond our control. The book is also dedicated to Chongba Sherpa, who passed away in the summer of 2017 after a short battle with cancer. Without him it would have been a different story.

ACKNOWLEDGEMENTS

Thanks to the other members of my Manaslu team – Anne-Mari, Ian, José, Karel, Mark, Mila, Robert, Robin and Steve – for being great company for many weeks.

Thanks to our amazing Sherpa team – including Chedar, Dorje, Kami, Pasang Gombu, Pasang Ongchu, Sangye, Tarke, and most of all Chongba – for their hard work and humility. It goes without saying that we could not have done it without their support.

Thanks to Phil Crampton for making it all happen.

Thanks to my editor, Alex Roddie, for his help polishing the text.

Most of all thanks to all of you, readers of my blog and diaries. I hope you have enjoyed this one, and I look forward to welcoming you back sometime. If you have not read it already then I hope you will enjoy my first full-length book, *Seven Steps from Snowdon to Everest*, about my ten-year journey from hill walker to Everest climber.

SEVEN STEPS FROM SNOWDON TO EVEREST

A hill walker's journey to the top of the world

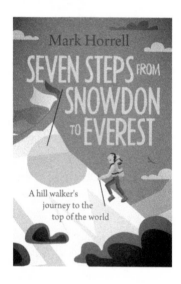

As he teetered on a narrow rock ledge a yak's bellow short of the stratosphere, with a rubber mask strapped to his face, a pair of mittens the size of a sealion's flippers, and a drop of two kilometres below him, it's fair to say Mark Horrell wasn't entirely happy with the situation he found himself in.

He was an ordinary hiker who had only read books about mountaineering, and little did he know when he signed up for an organised trek in Nepal with a group of elderly ladies that ten years later he would be attempting to climb the world's highest mountain.

But as he travelled across the Himalayas, Andes, Alps and East Africa, following in the footsteps of the pioneers, he dreamed up a seven-point plan to gain the skills and experience which could turn a wild idea into reality.

Funny, incisive and heartfelt, his journey provides a refreshingly honest portrait of the joys and torments of a modern-day Everest climber.

First published in 2015. A list of bookstores can be found on Mark's website:

www.markhorrell.com/SnowdonToEverest

PHOTOGRAPHS

I hope you enjoyed the photos in this book. Thanks to the miracles of the internet you can view all the photos from my Manaslu expedition online via the photo-sharing website *Flickr*.

Manaslu. Nepal, September to October, 2011:
www.markhorrell.com/Manaslu

ABOUT THE AUTHOR

Since 2010 Mark Horrell has written what has been described as one of the most credible Everest opinion blogs out there. He writes about trekking and mountaineering from the often silent perspective of the commercial client.

For over a decade he has been exploring the world's greater mountain ranges and keeping a diary of his travels. As a writer he strives to do for mountain history what Bill Bryson did for long-distance hiking.

Several of his expedition diaries are available as quick reads from the major online bookstores. His first full-length book, *Seven Steps from Snowdon to Everest*, about his ten-year journey from hill walker to Everest climber, was published in November 2015.

His favourite mountaineering book is *The Ascent of Rum Doodle* by W.E. Bowman.

ABOUT THIS SERIES

The *Footsteps on the Mountain Travel Diaries* are Mark's expedition journals. Quick reads, they are lightly edited versions of what he scribbles in his tent each evening after a day in the mountains.

For other titles in this series see Mark's website:
www.markhorrell.com/diaries

CONNECT

You can join Mark's **mailing list** to keep updated:
www.markhorrell.com/mailinglist

Website and blog: www.markhorrell.com
Twitter: @markhorrell
Facebook: www.facebook.com/footstepsonthemountain
Flickr: www.flickr.com/markhorrell
YouTube: www.youtube.com/markhorrell

DID YOU ENJOY THIS BOOK?

Thank you for buying and reading this book. Word-of-mouth is crucial for any author to be successful. If you enjoyed it then please consider leaving a review. Even if it's only a couple of sentences, it would be a great help and will be appreciated enormously.

Links to this book on the main online book stores can be found on Mark's website:

www.markhorrell.com/TheManasluAdventure

CPSIA information can be obtained
at www.ICGtesting.com
Printed in the USA
LVHW090518131118
596956LV00001B/121/P